END OF STORY

EN

D OF
STORY

toward an annihilation of
language and history

C R I S P I N   S A R T W E L L

STATE UNIVERSITY OF NEW YORK PRESS

Published by
STATE UNIVERSITY OF NEW YORK PRESS
ALBANY

For information, address
State University of New York Press,
90 State Street, Suite 700, Albany, NY 12207

Production and book design, Laurie Searl
Marketing, Anne Valentine

Library of Congress Cataloging-in-Publication Data

Sartwell, Crispin, 1958–
    End of story : toward an annihilation of language and history / Crispin Sartwell.
        p. cm.
    Includes bibliographical references and index.
    ISBN 0-7914-4725-1 (alk. paper) — ISBN 0-7914-4726-X (pbk. : alk. paper)
    1. Language and languages—Philosophy. I. Title.

P106 .S226 2000

                                                                            00-038769

            10   9   8   7   6   5   4   3   2   1

This book is for my son,

SAMUEL ABELL SARTWELL

I've lost the thread of the story I was telling.
My elephant roams his dream of Hindustan again.
Narrative, poetics, destroyed, my body,
a dissolving, a return.

—Rumi

The long waiting silence was utterly gone, the long tension—
a kind of grave, quiet anxiety with each man very much alone—
annihilated; and this was a continual enormously active present.

—Patrick O'Brian

Note, in the last left-hand example, how swiftly meaning
departs when words are wrongly juxtaposed.

—William Strunk and E. B. White

CONTENTS

ACKNOWLEDGMENTS

I'm very grateful to the Annenberg Scholars Program at the Annenberg School for Communication, University of Pennsylvania for providing a year to research this project and write it. Elihu Katz provided invaluable support and guidance, as did Barbara Grabias and my fellow scholars: Gene Burns, Michael Griffin, Dona Schwartz, and David Buckingham. The book originated in a series of arguments with Judith Bradford, and she also read and commented sharply on early versions of the manuscript. Margaret Urban Walker also read an early version and gave some valuable responses. Marion Winik read the manuscript with an effective bullshit detector and, in general, Marion Winik rocks. Thanks to Karmen MacKendrick for reading the manuscript and for being the coolest philosophy professor; her work and suggestions were an inspiration. And thanks to Glen Mazis for the intellectual and spiritual support. Bill Mahar and the School of Humanities at Penn State Harrisburg have been very helpful indeed in a variety of ways. Jane Bunker steered this book through shoals of piranha. Laurie Searl was wonderful to work with on the design. Parts of the book were presented at Smith College, the University of Alberta, and the Kansas City Art Institute, and I made substantive changes after the discussions. If any infelicities or downright howlers remain, I hope you will blame these people and institutions rather than me.

PUTTING LANGUAGE IN ITS PLACE

In Jorge Luis Borges's famous fable, the universe is a library. It consists of hexagonal rooms. On each wall of each room are five shelves holding thirty-five volumes each. Each volume in turn has four hundred and ten pages, each page forty lines. The library contains a single example of each possible volume-sized combination of the letters of the alphabet, the space, the comma, and the period. It appears to its inhabitants to be limitless, hexagons opening on hexagons further than one could wander in many lifetimes. And in such a lifetime one might not find a single coherent sentence, much less a great work of literature. Nevertheless, there are those who assert that every volume in the library makes sense in some language or other. This claim Borges refutes by pointing out that "four hundred and ten pages of inalterable MCVs cannot correspond to any language, no matter how dialectal or rudimentary it may be."[1]

Even in such a place, some concessions must be made to the human organism. Each hexagon contains two small closets: "In the first, one may sleep standing up; in the other, satisfy one's fecal necessities" (51). When one dies, letting go once and for all of the project of making sense out of the inalterable MCVs and the rest of the gobbledygook, one is pitched over the railing to fall through the books for eternity, or thereabouts.

---

1. Jorge Luis Borges, "The Library of Babel," *Labyrinths* (New York: New Directions, 1964), p. 53.

Ours is an era obsessed by language. Or it is better to say that ours is an academy obsessed by language. When we try to make sense or nonsense out of our world, our selves, or our institutions, we seem to do it in language and by means of the trope of language. Analytic philosophy used to be concerned with the question of how words refer to the world. Under the auspices of Wittgenstein, Quine, Rorty, and others this question has been more or less abandoned in favor of questions about the relations of words to one another; so Quine says that words do not refer at all except within a whole language, Wittgenstein that talking in general about word/world relations is impossible because it constitutes a language game that purports to stand outside all language games (philosophy), Rorty that we should stop talking about the world at all and rest content with multiplying texts. The hermeneutics of Gadamer and others takes the interpretation of texts as a model for all human experience, as if we lived indeed in a library in which every volume made sense in some language or other. Deconstructionists start with the axiom that there is nothing outside the text, an axiom that would be even more compelling than it is (though not, for all that, perfectly compelling) if we lived in the Library of Babel. More widely, a lot of folks (Bernard Williams and Martha Nussbaum, for instance) try to make sense of human life as narrative, or by means of narrative, or in terms of "constitutive life projects." They describe moral education or ethical life as requiring narrative, or they explain our values by means of stories and assert that those values require stories. Others, following Foucault, describe the sources of knowledge and truth as human power relations, which they in turn describe as modes of discourse. Some feminists and African-American theorists associate being oppressed with a condition in which one cannot tell or make one's own story, and describe their oppressors as engaged in the construction of meta- or master-narratives. Lyotard holds that such metanarratives are breaking down into a profusion of micronarratives. These are different approaches, but they have one thing in common: there's no escape from the scribble.

There is something to be said for all these positions. The project that conceives as fundamental the question of how words refer to the world is locked inside a more or less completely bad ontology (an ontology that distinguishes words from "real things"). Deconstruction does interesting things to texts. Stories are central to articulating lives and values. Bodies are indeed zones of inscription, and oppression and liberation both often involve configurations of narrative. It is obvious, furthermore, that those obsessed by language are involved in various disagreements: MacIntyre wants to reconstruct a master narrative; bell hooks wants to rip master narratives apart. Quine wants to account for the language of science; Rorty wants to develop alternatives to it.

Gadamer wants to understand the world as a library; Foucault wants to show us the pain that bodies endure as they are inscribed. Goodman says that worlds are made by symbol systems; Derrida displays how such worlds collapse under the weight of their own elisions.

But all these views set out from a single-minded concentration on language. Although language is used in many ways and for many purposes in contemporary academic discourse, the centrality or even ubiquity of language in human life is rarely questioned. This book is a discourse against discourse, a discourse that wants what all these thinkers omit: silence. Whereof one cannot speak, thereof one must be silent; but it is, I think, also possible to pass over in silence much of which we could speak. Indeed, all of us pass over almost everything in silence; even the greatest chatterer can say only so much, thank god.

Sporadically throughout this book, I will be speculating on the reasons for the obsession with language. Cutting to the chase, I think that this obsession emerges within the era of technology, an era in which our basic relations to the world and to other human beings are conceived technologically. The form of life that regards the world and other human beings as stuff to be used, to be transformed toward ends, is a form of life that I will call, in what follows, teleological. In some sense it is founded in the foundation of the West, in Aristotle's account of human action, and of the universe as a whole, as being directed toward ends, always and everywhere. Human action would, on Aristotle's account, be impossible outside a teleological order, and the fundamental explanation of any event turns on what the telos of that event is—at what end it is aiming.

My thesis is that this thought, while foundational of the Western tradition, has intensified to the point of monomania in this century. Alongside the analytic philosophy that got itself more and more lost in the library of Babel, there developed a theory of action that was utterly teleological. Alongside the hermeneutic tradition that affirmed the absolute hegemony of language as if it were a liberation, there developed a narratology that reduced everything to stories and that made stories definable in terms of *telos*. And alongside all of this, there developed an unprecedented technological environment in which all the world came to be conceived as consisting of resources, as an object for use. Technology has always been dedicated to the production of artificial environments, and the philosophies that make of life a story or a drama have coincided with the production of virtual environments in which everything organic is impertinent or expunged. Stories are things we tell; words are things we wield. If the world were a story and if we were words, the world and we would belong to ourselves; we would be the narrators of our world. In my opinion, even in the technologically transformed environment in which we live, and even as we live, transformed, within that environment, the notion that the world belongs to us and is the subject of our will is a sick fantasy, a megalomaniac delusion.

There is much to be said for "social constructionism": the idea that we and our world are made by common agreement or are produced by our languages and the various disciplinary procedures they subserve. Social constructionism is a hopeful doctrine because it allows us the belief that the things that cause us pain—racism and sexism, for example—can be transformed by a transformation in our language. There is, I am saying, truth in that. But it is the limits of the social construction of reality that I am going to trace in this book: the ways in which the world exceeds our grasp and in which we exceed our own grasp. There is hope there too, because though there is much that we can change and much that we must change, there is much that we can allow to be, and there is a joy or peace in allowing things to be. I hope that there are limits to the technological transformation of the environment and the technological transformation of ourselves, and I hope that there is the possibility of a post-technological epoch in which the basic questions are not, or not only, teleological. No doubt we have purposes. No doubt we must. But we also must let our purposes go, must find ways to make peace with our world instead of fantasizing a perfect conquest.

The discourses that grow out of the obsession with discourse occasionally bloat language into something really hideous, like a corpse that has floated two weeks in the East River. Occasionally the position is so overstated that it is (for my money) baldly ridiculous: if the assertion is that the world is a text, or people are texts, the assertion asserts what I daresay no one can actually believe. Try believing it when you stub your toe; try believing it at the moment of orgasm; try believing it while you undergo chemotherapy; try believing it in the wilderness or, for that matter, in a traffic jam. On the other hand, most of the thinkers discussed here are more thoughtful or at least less grandiose than that. But here I am more concerned with their omissions than with their commissions.

There is every reason in the world to enter into a detailed discussion of language games, or a detailed description and critique of master narratives, or a detailed prescription for retrieving meaning out of narratively articulated traditions. But what is left out in Foucault, Nussbaum, MacIntyre, Rorty, Quine, and Lyotard is the moment of silence, the moment of death, the moment of inarticulate orgasm. One way to make this point, which has been beautifully developed by Bataille, is to remind us of ecstasy: the extraordinary experience of letting-go into the divine, or into the lover, or into death: the extraordinary experience to which language seems radically insufficient. This movement is present in all great spiritual traditions (with regard to which it is often called "mysticism"), as when the *Tao Te Ching* says that the Tao that can be spoken is not the real Tao, or when the Zen master, asked for the one word of power, replies by burping.

I will be discussing such moments. But what I actually want to emphasize is what, in our everyday experience and in our everyday world, escapes linguistic articulation: at a rough estimate, almost everything. Try providing an exhaustive description of your own visual experience at any given moment, and you will see how much of what we experience, even if it could in principle be cast into language, isn't. Perhaps what we do frame into words in some sense constitutes our awareness at any given moment, though I hope not. If that is the case, then our awareness is a tiny chattering voice in the vast noise and the vast silence. This noise and silence make language necessary and are necessary to language. And although to bring them to awareness might consist of rendering them into words (though, I think, not only of that), we cannot, fortunately, be aware of everything at once. That is, some things (most things) always stand in excess to language, and it is this excess that drives us on linguistically, forces us into consciousness, and makes consciousness a continual burden and unconsciousness a continual threat.

Of course, I speak these words: *silence, death, noise, excess*. So I am saying what I am saying cannot be said. After all I am sucking everything right here into language. Rorty says: tell me about something outside language, and I'll believe you. Of course I might reply: tell me about everything, and *I* might believe *you*. Well, I just said it: "everything." Now *everything* is a good case for me, for it displays the total impoverishment of language in the face of the world as well as anything could. I just said everything, in the only way I know how, and what I just said amounts roughly to nothing. It is a little sound tossed up at a crushing universe, a tiny sign of the emptiness and impossible profusion out of which language emerges. Saying "everything" is saying nothing, and saying nothing can be a very good idea. For I'm not always talking. I can shut up. And if you demand that I stop talking about silence, then I will; I have. Eventually I pause for breath and fall silent, as do you. This book will end; I promise.

I am tortured by language. I speak to myself constantly; the "voice in my head" seems to me most of the time to be myself. I experience myself not as a body but as a speaker, a kind of hectoring lecturer always about the insufferable business of telling "my" body what to do. That is, I have a technological or teleological relation to myself. So when someone asserts that the human subject is a linguistic construction, I know only too well what she's talking about. But I spend a lot of time experiencing my need to escape from that notion of subjectivity.

I have constructed a little narrative of my life, where I come from and where I'm going, a narrative that takes me from rebellious child to Nobel laureate. I try to hold myself to that, but of course life is providing me all the time with interruptions to my ascent of the kind I should (but rarely do) expect. I've had trouble enough just getting a Ph.D. and an academic job, not to speak of the Nobel. Failing tests, getting drunk and falling over at parties, acting like a bona fide fool—these are the petty humiliations that mess up my little story. In fact, most of what happens to me and around me is incompatible with the arc of my walnut.

But the voice goes on: now needling, now howling, giving me no surcease at all from what Barthes, with touching optimism, termed "the rustle of language." I have engaged in years of expensive therapy, spent long periods of time in meditation, sucked down innumerable pounds of marijuana, all with the goal of *turning the damn thing off.* And folks are always calling me whenever I find a quiet moment. And my Nobel arc requires me to read and read and read, until words are coming out my ears. Writers such as Carolyn Heilbrun and Luce Irigaray have shown me that being without a language and without a voice are dangerous and debilitating things. But having nothing but a language and a voice is also a form of suffering, though perhaps not as deep or important a form of suffering. In any event, it is as a treatment for that form of suffering that I am writing this book.

Here are some quotations that set out a view that Rorty calls "textualism": the view, roughly, that the world (at least as it enters human experience or knowledge) and the self consist of text. Gadamer:

> Language is the fundamental mode of operation of our being-in-the-world and the all-embracing form of the constitution of the world.[2]

> [I]n all our knowledge of ourselves and in all knowledge of the world, we are always already encompassed by the language that is our own. We grow up, and we become acquainted with men and in the last analysis with ourselves when we learn to speak. . . . What is mad about [the idea that language has an extra-linguistic origin] is that [it wants] to suspend in some artificial way our very enclosedness in the linguistic world in which we live. In truth we are always already at home in language.[3]

---

2. Hans-Georg Gadamer, "The Universality of the Hermeneutical Problem," *Philosophical Hermeneutics* (Berkeley: University of California Press, 1976), p. 3.

3. Gadamer, "Man and Language," *Philosophical Hermeneutics*, pp. 62–63.

> Language is not a delimited realm of the speakable, over against which other realms that are not speakable might stand. Rather, language is all-encompassing. There is nothing that is fundamentally excluded from being said. (p. 67)

Nelson Goodman:

> If I ask about the world, you can offer to tell me how it is under one or more frames of reference; but if I insist that you tell me how it is apart from all frames, what can you say? We are confined to ways of describing whatever is described. Our universe, so to speak, consists of these ways rather than of a world.[4]

Rorty:

> What we know about both texts and lumps [physical objects] is nothing more than the ways these are related to the other texts and lumps mentioned in or presupposed by the propositions which we use to describe them.[5]

> [The good guys] believe that signs have meaning in virtue of their relations to other signs. . . . They further believe that all thought is in language, so that thoughts too have meaning only by virtue of their relations to other thoughts. For antilogocentrists, therefore, truth is not a matter of transparency to, or correspondence with, reality, but rather a matter of relating thoughts or signs to one another.[6]

I'm not going to try to refute all these claims or even worry about them particularly. Instead, I'm going to head out on a wandering that I hope will show something about what it's like to be trapped in language in various modalities and how we might get out, supposing that we want to. The point is not to show that the claims made in these quotations are false. Although I think they *are* false, I also think that they cannot be shown to be false; every such refutation would be a linguistic item and would finally only tend to confirm what it attacked. The question here is: what do such claims show about the form of life of the people who make them, and what does the fact that I understand that way of life only too well show about the way I am living?

---

4. Nelson Goodman, *Ways of Worldmaking* (Indianapolis: Hackett, 1978), p. 3.

5. Rorty, "Texts and Lumps," *Objectivity, Relativism, and Truth* (New York: Cambridge University Press, 1991), p. 88.

6. Rorty, "De Man and the American Cultural Left," *Essays on Heidegger and Others* (New York: Cambridge University Press, 1991), p. 130.

I'm going to explore that form of life in particular with regard to the experience it encodes or the desires it embodies with regard to time and to history. I will try to relate these claims to what, again, is a characteristically Western madness: a mania for the teleological ordering of time and of the lives that take place in time. So there is a genealogy here. But my strategy, finally, is not argumentative; it is to confront these thinkers with their own experience and to confront you with your own experience and ask over and over: do you really believe this? what would it be like to believe it? what does it mean about you that you want to believe it? what is omitted from your belief, and why do you want or need to omit it? What I want you to hear above all is the howl—the visceral rejection of this form of life by someone who has experienced it too thoroughly. What I want to do is display this visceral rejection and make you feel its force. The howl itself is inarticulate; it is not a sign of anything, it is a sonic and existential event. If there could be a book that was a sheer howl, I would try to write it, but instead this book I am actually going to write will itself prowl among texts; this book I am going to write is itself locked into the order of the sign and into the teleological order. This book displays my entrapment in language as clearly as anything could, and in that sense it confirms what it attacks. But in that sense too the attack is redoubled, or the need for the attack is made all the more obvious: this book is the disease I am trying to treat; it tries to cure itself above all. I am the person farthest away from the cure that I myself prescribe; this book is an attack on myself, on itself, a structure devoted to its own annihilation.

So I want to try to develop or discover ways out of the linguistic and narrative teleological order in which this development and discovery are all the while embedded. I want to bring you some relief, if you need or want relief, and I want to show you why I need relief and how I try to find it. This book does not speak to the condition of being deprived of language or narrative; this book does not speak for the silenced. It speaks to the voice, writes at the writer, tries to cure not the oppressed but the oppressor. Whether the oppressor's oppression of himself is an artifact of his oppression of others, or whether his oppression of others is an artifact of his oppression of himself, I am addressing the oppression of the oppressor by himself; I am addressing my own self-division and self-control. And what I am aiming at by the hopeless means of further self-oppression is not just relief, but finally, *release*; I want to grope toward a release from regimes of signs, to release myself into a place where I can have my everyday life without remaking it into a narrative, and I want to offer strategies of release to you if you want them.

CHAPTER ONE

TELOS AND TORTURE

I

Many recent thinkers have held that human lives are lived largely in or through narratives. Advocates of this view maintain, in one form or another, that our self-understandings and our understandings of others are articulated as stories. And they tend to connect this alleged fact with the alleged human drive for meaning, a drive that pulls us back from the abyss where death by suicide beckons.

Narrative has become a sort of philosophical panacea, performing all sorts of tasks that philosophers and other intellectuals seem to think need performing. Narrative has been used, for example, to explain the human experience of time. It has been used in the personal existential project of constructing a coherent life out of the chaos of experience; here, it sorts for relevance and yields explanations. It has been used to describe or explain the forms human sociality, to develop a taxonomy of roles or archetypes. It has been used as a central ethical category, or as a ground for ethical theory.

All these functions have something in common. In each case, narrative is a principle of or a strategy for organization. Narrative gives form, or displays form, or imposes form. This should hardly be surprising. In its use with regard to drama, the epic, and the novel—the use from which it has been expanded—narrative is the most general term to express the sheer fact that the work is organized. When we say that narrative is what makes possible the human experience of time, for example, we may well mean that it organizes time, which may in turn mean that it brings order out of a chaotic temporal flow, or that it makes an experience of time for the first time possible, that in

9

some sense it makes time. And likewise narrative is supposed to be a principle or a category for displaying or constructing forms of organization in lives, social systems, or axiomatics.

The other central distinguishing feature of narrative in all its uses is that it lends meaning to what is organized under its auspices. The notion of narrative was developed with regard to literary artifacts. The primary notion of meaning is what emerges within the interpretation of such objects. What is paradigmatically "meaningful" is the linguistic structure or work; its meaning can perhaps be given in an interpretation which correlates its units with other linguistic units, or with experiences, or with objects in the world. If it turned out that human life were narrative, or that time and the world in time were experienced fundamentally as narrative, human life would be an appropriate object for this sort of interpretation. Human life would have "meaning" in as straightforward a sense as anything can have meaning.

I will be attempting something of a genealogy and a therapy for such views. I will try to sketch the limits of narrative as a category, and some of its political sources and implications. I'm going to run serially through several philosophers on these matters, probing for a way out of their narratives, out of my narratives, out of all narratives. I will question whether and to what extent human experience and human life are organized narratively, and I will question whether human experience and human life are meaningful, what that might mean, and why we seem to think they should be, or that we would commit suicide if they were not.

This is not to say that narrative doesn't have liberatory possibilities, and it not to say that I or you could or should live without it. But I will share with you that I believe that every counter-narrative brings with it a new capacity of oppression, and that this capacity is proportional to the coherence and meaningfulness of the narrative. So the more narrativized the narrative, the more thoroughly organized and chock-full of significance it is, the more problematic. I am interested, then, not only in departures from narrative, or in letting go of narrative, but also in the ways narratives are compromised as narratives in narratives, the ways they break down, evade paraphrase, incorporate and are incorporated by the random, provide us with lines of flight from themselves and from ourselves.

A particularly clear version of the uses of narrative I will be rejecting has been put forward by Alasdair MacIntyre. At the outset, however, I want to emphasize that not all narrativism can be tarred with the brush with which I paint MacIntyre, as we shall see. Nevertheless, MacIntyre's position is useful as an initial stalking horse. He writes:

> I am what I may justifiably be taken by others to be in the course
> of living out a story that runs from my birth to my death; I am the
> subject of a history that is my own and no one else's, that has its
> own peculiar meaning. When someone complains—as do some of
> those who attempt or commit suicide—that his or her life is mean-
> ingless, he or she is often and perhaps characteristically complain-
> ing that the narrative of their life has become unintelligible to
> them, that it lacks any point, any movement toward a climax or
> telos. Hence the point of doing any one thing rather than another
> at crucial junctures in their lives seems to such a person to have
> been lost.[1]

Here we have a version of narrative as existential project, which MacIntyre
connects quite correctly to forms of social organization and comprehension.

MacIntyre places stringent criteria of unity on what could count as a narrative; for his purposes, life as narrative first off requires a telos toward which
that life is driving, and secondly organizes the events of that life fairly strictly
with regard to that telos.

> In what does the unity of an individual life consist? The answer is that
> its unity is the unity of a narrative embodied in a single life. . . . The
> unity of a human life is the unity of a narrative quest. Quests some-
> times fail, are frustrated, abandoned, or dissipated into distractions;
> and human lives may in all these ways also fail. But the only criteria
> for success or failure in a human life as a whole are the criteria of suc-
> cess or failure in a narrated or to-be-narrated quest. (218–19)

For MacIntyre, then, narrative is bound up with the teleology of human life, a
teleology that lends life intelligibility or makes it meaningful. Life is something
at which we can succeed or fail, and the standards of success or failure are given
with reference to a goal; progress toward or regress away from that goal yields
standards for evaluation of lives. "The meaning of life" is then the goal toward
which your life or even all human life tends; the "story" of your life is the story
of progress toward or regress away from that goal.

This teleological emphasis emerges directly from Aristotle, although the
view that teleology and narrative are identical cannot be attributed to him. But
recall the opening of the *Nicomachean Ethics*:

> Every craft and every investigation, and likewise every action and
> decision, seems to aim at some good; hence the good has been well
> described as that at which everything aims. . . . Suppose, then, that

---

1. *After Virtue* (Notre Dame: Notre Dame University Press, 2nd edition 1984), p.
217.

(a) there is some end of the things we pursue in our actions which we wish for because of itself and because of which we wish for the other things; and (b) we do not choose everything because of something else, since (c) if we do, it will go on without limit, making desire empty and futile; then clearly (d) this end will be the good, i.e., the best good.[2]

Part of my point in what follows is that far from representing a series of trivial truths or tautologies, this view is, at the time Aristotle proposes it, an innovation, and that, at any time, it is optional: it describes a particular form of life, and one that is not even very thoroughly pursued in the cultures in which it has currency. For now, however, note that we have an arrangement or distribution of projects, and that this distribution is determined by an overarching telos (I will call this distribution in what follows the *teleological order*). This arrangement of projects subsumes, for Aristotle, all the crafts and arts, all investigations, all actions, all decisions, and finally, all things. Thus, it is the teleological order that first articulates the arena of all human active and even mental life, and it is also this order which in some sense connects human life to the cosmos, which is itself organized teleologically. Consider, for example, the fundamental notion of 'final cause' in Aristotle: the basic mode of explanation even of nonhuman nature is teleological. "[T]he science which knows to what end each thing must be done is the most authoritative of the sciences, and more authoritative than any ancillary science; and this end is the good in each class, and in general the supreme good in the whole of nature."[3] So there is an order of nested teleologies in which human lives must find a place; to find the place of human life in that order is to compose an "ethics." And notice too that the initially quoted passage betrays the anxiety that a life lived in local ends, life without an overarching project that subsumes the others, would be "empty and futile."

Then the immediate role of ethics is to provide an account of practical reasoning: that is, a strategy or technique by which we can display the ordering of human action for ends. First, such account will (supposedly) be descriptive: it will show how we actually (supposedly) go about ordering our actions by ends. And then it will also be normative: it will show which ends are worthy of pursuit. So it will simultaneously provide us with self-understanding within the teleological order and make us better or more excellent agents within that

---

2. Aristotle, *Nicomachean Ethics*, trans. Terence Irwin (Indianapolis: Hackett, 1985), pp. 1, 2.

3. Aristotle, *Metaphysics* 982b, trans. W. D. Ross in *The Complete Works of Aristotle*, vol. 2 (Princeton: Princeton University Press, 1985), p. 1554.

order. It will describe the "meaning" of life in the narrativist sense and help us to realize that meaning. It will, thus, by sketching a limit, show us how lives (significantly, womanish or slavish lives) can fail in this order or be located outside it. And it will connect meaningful and excellent lives to a cosmic order that itself is driving toward ends in which our projects themselves participate.

It is problematic to assert that there are any criteria for the success and failure of whole lives, much less to assume blandly that we need such criteria or have access to them. It would be worth asking: why do we want to evaluate whole lives for success or failure? What does that practice indicate about the sorts of people that get constructed in particular situations? I think that such a genealogy, of which I will give a sketch in later sections, would have to proceed through an understanding of political or economic contexts that would make such evaluations possible and important. It is significant, that is, just who Aristotle excludes from this order. If life has a goal, then we can evaluate lives for their success or failure, but think for a moment of how problematic such evaluations are. "Her life was a failure." What would that mean? That she didn't have children, or that she didn't rise to the top of her profession, or that she was unhappy, or that she made other people unhappy, or that she didn't achieve salvation? Think first of all of how problematic any particular evaluation to that effect is. And think very carefully about what social practices would demand or make use of such evaluations, and about whether there could be social practices that did not. I am not certain that life has a goal. I could live with that, and am living with it anyhow, since if my life has a goal, I have no idea what it is. Now, on the other hand, I am not so certain I could live with having a life-goal, and eventually I will try to explain why.

It would seem that a life could be narrated from an indefinite number of points of view internal and external to the person whose life is being narrated. These are going to be related because, as we will see, MacIntyre thinks that narratives are constructed socially, so that insofar as the various narrative agencies are embedded in the same sociality, their sense of relevance and articulation of goals will likely be similar (at a minimum, they will present lives with the same taxonomy of meanings and purposes). From an external point of view, a life that is dissipated in distractions from its quest is perfectly narratable; it is narrated as a failure. But consider for a moment what such a life is like from the inside, if it is self-conscious and narratively constructed. To be dissipated into distractions is to lose track of one's goals, to flounder around among goals, or without clear goals. By MacIntyre's account, that would be an experience of the breakdown of narrative, though one would still be "living in a narrative" to the extent that there is a socially articulated telos from which one is distracted.

The lapse into unintelligibility from the internal point of view of which MacIntyre speaks—the dissipation into distraction, and so forth—must by MacIntyre's own lights be a breakdown in the ability to find a narrative for oneself, to connect with the ongoing stories provided by one's culture. For MacIntyre, life as a quest story is life as a project. The project might fail of completion, or one might be distracted from one's quest, and so forth. But the experience of the loss of project itself must be an abandonment of the narrative from the internal point of view.

> We live out our lives, both individually and in our relationships with each other, in the light of certain conceptions of a possible shared future. . . . There is no present which is not informed by some image of some future and an image of the future which always presents itself in the form of a telos—or of a variety of ends or goals—toward which we are either moving or failing to move in the present. (215–16)

Here, MacIntyre strikes the theme of narrative as the experience of temporality. But he gives this a particularly emphatic spin; for MacIntyre, the human experience of time involves the organization of current energies with regard to a determinate imagined future. This is in turn related to the Aristotelian conception of practical rationality, so that we derive an account of temporality from an ethical "insight": we are located in time insofar as we organize the past and perform acts of will in the present in the service of or with regard to a determinate telos or a determinate plurality of purposes. The human form of temporality is the quest narrative or the project; lives can then be evaluated from the point of view of their goals; temporality is rationality is narrative; we are smeared over time by the use of ourselves or our bodies as our own instruments or as the instruments of others. The possibility of a breakdown of intelligibility would hence, for MacIntyre, be a breakdown in goals, a moment, for example, in which the present ceases to be informed by an image of the future, or in which the present ceases to be dedicated instrumentally to the service of the future, in which the past ceases to be "read" as a story of the application of a series of past presents to past, present, and future futures. To lapse into such a moment (if it is possible, according to MacIntyre, to do so) would be to lapse not into an unintelligible narrative; rather, it would be to lapse into the realm of the unnarrated. Or more precisely, that is how it would appear from the point of view of the "distracted" person.

That is why I say that MacIntyre imposes rather draconian constraints of coherence on narratives. A life or a life-slice constitutes for MacIntyre a narrative just insofar as that life or segment is organized instrumentally with regard to purposes, so that any material that resists such organization, that cannot be smoothly taken up into the temporality constructed in instrumental rationality, compromises the coherence of the narrative, which is to say that it compromises the narrative character of the life in question. Of course, it is amazing what can be incorporated into a narrative; what seems to evade or compromise the narrative gets incorporated as a barrier or a distraction or a lapse, and hence appears precisely within the narrative. The capacity of narrative as MacIntyre understands it to organize a life is very great indeed. On the other hand, as I will suggest, one could work this the other way round; one might assert that even the most coherent narrative is already compromised, has already broken down, is already in excess to instrumentality.

To repeat, one might, particularly from the external point of view, easily enough sweep up moments that evade or obstruct coherence into a narrative: "Then for a moment, lost in the throes of orgasm, he ceased to order his life by goals." On the other hand, we have arrived at what seems to be a standoff, for one might also start sweeping whole lives into unintelligibility; one might regard the prodigious effort to order one's life into a series of projects, which are in turn ordered into a single project, as the desperate imposition of a comprehensible surface on a massive incomprehensible randomness. (It is perhaps this view—the view that there is prenarrative experience or a random world which precedes narrative organization—that MacIntyre most firmly rejects; he diagnoses it as a symptom of modernity or as existential romanticism. And all the textualists I mentioned earlier—Rorty, say, or Goodman—likewise oppose this view as strongly as they oppose anything; they point out that we cannot hold up the prelinguistic world for comparison with the linguistic articulation of the world; the world comes to be in its articulations into language, or really just is a system of symbols, and so on.) Every lapse or distraction can be narrated from some point of view, but on the other hand every narrative is also lapsing or distracted. The lapse of goal can appear within the narrative, but it appears precisely as a lapse, as an interstice in the narrative structure. One might indicate the relation of a particular event as a lapse to the order of teleology. But one might also ostend or celebrate the moments in the narrative in which the narrative is coming apart, is in danger of lapsing into incoherence or meaninglessness, in which goals shift or dissolve, or in which one ceases at a certain moment to order one's life in terms of a projected future.

I've tried to live my own life with an extreme degree of coherence; I've tried to understand my own life as a techne, to dedicate it to the realization of well-defined goals. I've tried to rationalize my life: both to live it rationally and to convince myself that I have lived or am living it rationally. I reached a point at which I came to experience the need to do that as a torture. I came to experience the recalcitrance of myself to my will, came to experience the immensity of my own horrible and lovely irrationality. I came also to experience or to admit the recalcitrance of the world to my will. The latter recalcitrance I could initially narrate as a series of "barriers" to my life-plan. But I reached the point at which I wanted to learn to let the world be instead of trying to transform it into an instrument of my will. So, as I say, we are in a standoff here, a standoff between the future and the present, between rationality and ecstasy, between meaning and affirmation.

MacIntyre takes this standoff and actually uses it as an argument for his position. He quotes one of Samuel Johnson's travel diaries which appears to report, in the quaint current phrase, that life is "just one damned thing after another." (You might have noticed this: your life, most days, *is* just one damned thing after another, and you're too tired, at day's end, to work up any of it, much less, ludicrously, all of it in relation to your quest.): "There we waited on the ladies—Morville's.—Spain. Country towns all beggars. At Dijon he could not find the way to Orleans.—Cross roads of France very bad.—Five soldiers.—Women.—Soldiers escaped . . . etc. etc." Johnson's stuff looks like just a fragmentary set of specific observations with no attempt to impose a connective flow, much less a narrative coherence. Oddly, MacIntyre twists this into an argument for his own position. He remarks that "the characterization of actions allegedly prior to any narrative form being imposed upon them will always turn out to be the presentation of what are plainly the disjointed parts of some possible narrative" (215). No doubt we could suck all of Johnson's observations into a narrative if there were any profit in so doing. On the other hand, and as I will discuss presently, we could also try to show how narratives themselves fail of coherence, how every characterization of actions allegedly ordered into the structures of plot will always turn out to be radically in excess of any possible narrative. Every narrative is just as plainly slapped together from bits of a possible randomness. "Unintelligible actions are failed candidates for the status of intelligible actions" (209), MacIntyre writes. But intelligible actions are, by the same token, not exhausted by their intelligibility, and are radically amputated by the desperation with which intelligibility is imposed on them. What might be true to say is that narrative coherence and chaos are mutually and simultaneously caused and that the experience of each is impossible without the experience of the other. So I yearn for the prenarrative or what exceeds narrative precisely as an expression of the thoroughness with which my life is narrated; I engage in a romantic yen for the "primitive" or the ateleological. But then the dialectic runs just as firmly the other way: there is a desperation in the thoroughness with which narrative is made in experience.

To anticipate, it is worth remarking that there are narratives that boil down to a series of apparently disconnected moments, that thematize precisely this disconnection as a way of collapsing writer and reader back into the unfolding present. Perhaps the greatest example of this is Bashō's *Okyu-no-hosomichi*, which is the tale of a pilgrimage, in other words an example of a primary narrative form, the there-and-back-again travelogue familiar in the west since the *Odyssey*. But here is a passage, in Cyd Corman's translation:

> Spent night at Iizuka, bathed at hot-springs, found lodgings but only thin mats over bare earth, ramshackle sort of place. No lamp, bedded down by shadowy light of fireplace and tried to get some rest. All night, thunder, pouring buckets, roof leaking, fleas mosquitoes in droves: no sleep. . . . Hired horses, got to post town of Ko-ori. Future seemed further off than ever, and recurring illness nagged, but what a pilgrimage to far places calls for: willingness to let world go, its momentariness, to die on the road, human destiny, which lifted spirit a little, finding foot again here and there, crossing the Okido Barrier in Date.[4]

This passage raises many themes that we will explore as time goes on, including destiny. But for now, notice that momentariness, in contrast to the temporal smear of narrative, is the theme of this passage and is also instantiated in it; the book as a whole offers a series of lessons in reawakening to the present moment. The *Okyu-no-hosomichi* is a narrative that displays the fact that narratives, as also lives, are constructed out of a series of presences or presents, so that though we build moments into narrative, the narrative also disintegrates into moments. Of course Bashō's primary literary form is the haiku, which is always devoted to bringing the moment home, to crystallizing an instant:

> Rainwater clings to
> the quartz pebble, and to me.
> Briefly, we glisten.

My only complaint about the haiku as a poetic form is that it is too long.

I am not sure whether MacIntyre believes that human life as quest or as project could be abandoned, for he believes that lives take place within social practices, and that social practices provide those lives with goals. But here are a few bald assertions. No human life has ever been ordered with the degree of coherence that MacIntyre ascribes to every human life. The quest is only one

---

4. Bashō, *Back Roads to Far Towns*, trans. Cyd Corman and Kamaike Susumu (Hopewell, NJ: Ecco Press, 1996), p. 61.

particular form of narrative and itself reflects a certain very specific social positioning. One can be driven to suicide by the lapse into unintelligibility, but one can also be driven to suicide by the attempt to render the incredible welter and incoherent profusion of a life perfectly intelligible. And even the suicide by unintelligibility may respond to the socially articulated demand to make oneself intelligible.

A useful example here is the Book of Job. Job loses a sense of narrative coherence in his life as he loses the things and people he loves. Above all, he loses the teleological ordering of his life; one senses that he always assumed that faith and righteousness would be rewarded, thus that he deserved the things and the happiness and the children that he had, and that, furthermore, he would continue to have them or indeed to accumulate them. God allows Satan to try Job's faith by ripping Job's neat little story of his life to shreds, by taking away the teleological order, by stripping every project and every purpose from Job except the one remaining, highest purpose: to serve God and keep faith. Job's response is what I would call "ecstatic": the prose of the King James version loses structure, just pours:

> My days are swifter than a weaver's shuttle, and are spent without hope. O remember that my life is wind: mine eye shall no more see good. The eye of him that hath seen me shall see me no more: thine eyes are upon me, and I am not. As the cloud is consumed and vanisheth away: so he that goeth to the grave shall come up no more. . . . My soul chooseth strangling, and death rather than my life. I loathe it; I would not live alway. . . . How long wilt thou not depart from me, nor let me alone till I swallow down my own spittle. . . . And why dost thou not pardon my transgression, and take away mine iniquity? for now I shall sleep in the dust; and thou shalt seek me in the morning, but I shall not be. (Job 7)

Job here longs to be relieved not only of his trials and of his life, but of God. He yearns not for a glorious afterlife, but for absolute extinction ("as the cloud is consumed and vanisheth away"); that is why I call the passage ecstatic, for there are ecstasies of pain as well as of pleasure, and the seduction to ecstasy is always also a seduction to extinction.

Now this lamentation could be read, in fact is most naturally read, in a way that MacIntyre would find compatible with his ethics. Job has "lost the thread of the story he was telling"; he's lost the things and the purposes that give his life meaning. When he loses these things, he comes to yearn for extinction, and this yearning is itself narrated ("as the cloud is consumed and vanisheth away"): narrated precisely as the "lapse," the "barrier," the "distraction" from project. Job might as well be extinguished at this point if the project cannot be resuscitated, if God will not finally reinstate the teleological order, will not again make sense of Job's faith. Job's despair could then be represented as a despair arising from the loss of narrative meaning. Indeed, this world and his own life no longer make sense to Job along the neat lines that they did previously: that God rewards righteousness with earthly happiness, and thus that the life of an exemplary man of faith will be a linear progress toward and in happiness.

But I want to suggest a different reading, one that is, oddly enough, compatible with what I am speculating MacIntyre's reading would be. We could represent the instrument of Job's torment alternately as his loss of narrative or as the narrative itself. What drives Job to despair is his loss of meaning, but what makes him sensible of that loss is precisely the meaningful ordering of his life. Job has achieved a perfect, effortless conciliation with the teleological order: that is the sense (here) in which he is the man of faith. He has expunged himself perfectly (or apparently so) into the order of signs, into God's word. ("There was a man in the land of Uz, whose name was Job; and that man was perfect and upright, and one that feared God, and eschewed evil" [Job 1].) In that sense, the extinction he longs for is something that he already had; there was (apparently) nothing left of Job but the word of God: no excess, no disobedience, no tension. That is precisely why Satan wants to torment him. What drives Job to despair is the lapse, the failure of his narrative; his life has become incomprehensible in the teleological order ("as a cloud is consumed and vanishes away"). But that failure is, of course, only a failure by the standards of that order: ecstasy is only transgression where the symbolic order is installed. It is only a complete transgression where that order is installed perfectly, as it is in Job. The lack of meaning drives one toward extinction only insofar as meaning itself is experienced as an imperative. So it is as true to say that Job is driven to despair by faith as that he is driven to despair by a trial of faith, that he is as driven by the symbolic order as by its lapse. In fact, those are two ways of saying the same thing.

And I am interested in the prose here, for it is a disintegration of sense inscribed precisely within the word of God. The passage I quoted is the hub or pivot of the Book of Job; it is a longing for extinction expressed precisely in a process of the extinction of sense ("my life is wind . . . and I am not"). In that sense the passage is ecstatic—"my life is wind . . . and I am not"—that is what ecstasy is, what defies and extinguishes the narrative order. That is the moment at which Satan's trial comes to a certain kind of fruition: Job does not even doubt God's providence, but he wants to be annihilated from the order of that providence, if *this* is the form it takes. It is important that this desire for, or indeed experience of, annihilation can be taken up into the order of signs ("my life is wind . . . and I am not"): that confirms MacIntyre's vision of that order. But it is equally important that it *is* a desire for annihilation that is so taken up ("my life is wind . . . and I am not"): that disarticulates the order of signs within that very order. You could not have this narrative without the moment of its disarticulation, and you could not have the moment of disarticulation without the narrative. The excess must be *inscribed*, the order must be reinstated. But the *excess* must be inscribed; the order must be compromised. The narrative is an exercise in intelligibility, but for that very reason it feeds off unintelligibility, needs it as it expunges it.

God shatters Job's practical rationality. Or better, he shatters the world in which practical rationality is possible or in which sense itself makes sense. God shows to Job a world in which actions have no predictable consequences, in which there is no moral order whatever as any of us might be given to understand it. That shattering, surrendered to, *is* Job's liberation, his enlightenment, his "return." And that universe is *our* universe, a universe which displays no moral order that we can understand. When, as in Aristotle and Hegel, human action is linked in the teleological order to the unfolding of the world, the world is made comically human—comically because even human beings aren't arranged and don't arrange things teleologically very often or very well. The basic insight is right: we are linked to the world's order (and its chaos); we are the world's order (and its chaos) in one of its manifestations. But we need to take the shattering inhumanity of that order and try to understand ourselves within it or surrender ourselves to it, rather than trying to take our imposition of order on ourselves and one another as a model for the universe.

When God speaks to Job from the whirlwind, he speaks as a whirlwind would speak if whirlwinds spoke; he speaks in an overwhelming advocacy of chaos. He says: do you think I made the world for *you*, little man; do you think I made the world even for human beings?

> Is the wild ox willing to serve you? Will it spend the night in your
> crib? Can you tie it in the furrow with ropes, and will it harrow the
> valley after you? Will you depend on it because its strength is great,
> and will you hand over your labor to it? Do you have faith that it
> will return and bring grain to your threshing floor? (Job 39, New
> Revised Standard Version)

God displays for Job a creation that is not centered on the human, a world in which human teleology is dwarfed in a universe that pays it no heed whatever, that displays no order that corresponds to it.

> Who hath divided a watercourse for the overflowing of waters, or
> a way for the lightning of thunder; to cause it to rain on the earth,
> where no man is; on the wilderness, wherein there is no man; to
> satisfy the desolate and waste ground; and to cause the bud of the
> tender herb to spring forth? Hath the rain a father? (Job 38)

As Stephen Mitchell points out, Job and the reader are not meant to *answer* that
question; it sits there as a question, puncturing our pretensions to comprehension. Get used to bewilderment. Is there one single thing in this universe that
you can grasp adequately or fully? The world is brute and brutal, incomprehensible by any ethics; animals are ripping themselves apart at God's behest.

> Wilt thou hunt the prey for the lion? or fill the appetite of the
> young lions, when they couch in their dens, and abide in the covert
> to lie in wait? Who provideth for the raven his food? when his
> young ones cry unto God, they wander for lack of meat. (Job 38)

This God is the God of ravens no less than of men of virtue, and men of virtue
are carrion. The Book of Job gives the most radical answer imaginable in the-
ology to the problem of evil: God is the God of evil; God is the God of predation and of the corpse left to rot as much as of the good man of Uz. God is
the whirlwind that disarticulates your little moral structure. If God tests you it
is to break your comfortable little rationality so that you can find some measure of contact with reality.

What nails this brutal and beautiful cosmology is the image in verses 40
and 41 of the behemoth and the leviathan. *The New Oxford Annotated Bible*
describes these as symbols of chaos.[5] "Behold now behemoth, which I made
with thee" (40). (NRSV: "which I made just as I made you.") Here, God connects the creation of man with the creation of chaos; he connects human life
not to the order of the universe as in the wistful rationalisms of Aristotle and
Hegel, but to its disorder, its brutality, its predation, its love of killing. Consider
the passage about warhorses at 39, which is followed by this:

> Doth the hawk fly by thy wisdom, and stretch her wings toward the
> south? Doth the eagle mount up at thy command, and make her
> nest on high? She dwelleth and abideth on the rock, upon the crag
> of the rock, and the strong place. From thence she seeketh her prey,
> and her eyes behold afar off. Her young ones also suck up blood:
> and where the slain are, there is she.

---

5. *The New Oxford Annotated Bible* (New York: Oxford University Press, 1994), pp.
670n and 671n.

The message of Job, finally, is that you cannot break or tame the world; you cannot understand it (and if you could it would drive you insane); God's creation is not compassed in your moral order. The behemoth and the leviathan are, finally, the universe, are, finally, Job himself and God himself.

> Canst thou draw out leviathan with an hook? or his tongue with a cord which thou lettest down? Canst thou put an hook into his nose? or bore his jaw through with a thorn? Will he make supplications unto thee? will he speak soft words unto thee? Will he make a covenant with thee? wilt thou take him for a servant for ever? Wilt thou play with him as with a bird? or wilt thou bind him for thy maidens? (Job 41)

No deals; no answers. Let go.

The moment of letting go is the moment simultaneously of despair and of ecstasy. I think it is impossible to imagine ecstasy at all in human life as MacIntyre conceives human life. The moment of ecstasy is a moment of vertigo, a vertigo that responds to letting go of one's projects into an all-encompassing present moment. A life with a telos, if there were any such lives, would be a life in which moments of ecstasy are useless; they don't drive the quest anywhere; they suck you back from the grail to where you are now. But Job needs the ecstasy just as he needs the reinstatement of the theocentric order, disarticulated by Satan precisely at the behest of God. Every quest incorporates and seeks to expunge ecstasy: Gawaine was tempted to abandon the quest when he found an enchanted castle full of beautiful women; he faced the choice between ecstasy and project.

Of course, one might imagine the great pleasure of actually finding the grail, or of coming across another vision of or clue to its whereabouts; one might even call that ecstasy, I guess. On the other hand, MacIntyre, like Aristotle, holds that the quest is completed only at death, which might make you wonder if it is a quest for death, since that's its "end." We might say that Job's quest ceases to be a quest for happiness and becomes a quest precisely for death. But what I am going to suggest is that in some sense, by the internal logic of the quest, every quest is a quest for annihilation. The success of the quest only gets evaluated from the point of view external to the quester in question. Of course, if the quest is a quest for death, it's a also a quest to end one's thinking of one's life as a quest, and if life were the sort of unity that MacIntyre supposes it is, death would be a very great relief. At least you can let go of your little project at that point; no one, not even yourself, expects you to accomplish something today if you croaked last night, and the list you made for yourself of things to do tomorrow appears in the clothing of irony to those who discover it next to your corpse. Death is an "ecstasy" in that sense; the dead do not organize their lives around the future and what they're going to accomplish there.

Obviously, MacIntyre and Aristotle do not conceive the telos of a human life to be death, though that's its "end" in one sense. But the quest of which human life is supposed to consist is not like the grail quest, which could get accomplished within your life, thus confronting you with the question of what the hell to do next. MacIntyre's quest must suffice for an entire life, or it will not provide criteria for evaluation of lives. There can be and will be subquests, local goals to be met, and so on. But recall that MacIntyre is interested in giving an account of the unity of entire human lives and expects narrative to provide that. He cannot, thus, remain satisfied with piecemeal projects, local instrumentalities, a decent degree of temporally localized rationality. On the contrary, narrative must provide the socially articulated rational principles on which whole lives can be displayed in their coherence. I suppose discharging one's quest would under such circumstances be the worst possible fate; one would lapse into unintelligibility. One might as well commit suicide at *that* point. One suspects, of course, that there's going to be a place beyond death where all this gets sorted out; God will call you to judgment and tell you how you did on your project, grade you and write you a letter of recommendation.

And now let me frame a dilemma. If we take seriously MacIntyre's claim that the quest suffices for a life, and if we restrict our view to this life, then the quest can never be fulfilled, in which case human life (which just is, without remainder, quest), is perfectly futile. The alternative would be that the goal is to be reached or not reached in the next life, in which case human existence looks to me like an eternal torment, since I am tortured by project. Heaven in such a case looks exactly like hell.

MacIntyre is reticent about the next life, and of course Aristotle had a similar view without moving into the next life; essentially he believed that the goal was a life of action in accordance with virtue (action of the soul, embodied in study), and hence that by realizing the local goals one would eventually be accounted happy. So let's back off again into this life as a quest. The form of one's quest, the final narration of one's life, must be put into the hands of others; they'll use it in your eulogy. And they'll use it to order or explain their own lives and the lives they make together within social practices. Your life will then be, as indeed it has already been, part of their projects.

Thus, the telos of a human life has to be given within social practices, and for MacIntyre this means that the telos of human life is given by the roles one performs within those practices.

> I am someone's son or daughter, someone else's cousin or uncle; I
> am a citizen of this or that city, a member of this or that guild or
> profession. I belong to this clan, that tribe, this nation. Hence what
> is good for me has to be good for one who inhabits those roles. (220)

Indeed, the notion of role is central to MacIntyre's narrativization of human life.
"There is no 'I' apart from these [roles]" (176), MacIntyre writes, and the roles,
though they are determined by social practices, are conceived as dramatic per-
formances. MacIntyre goes so far as to order social interactions such as conver-
sations, as well as whole human lives, into literary genres. Now one could easily
nudge this into absurdity. But for now I just want to appeal to your self-reflec-
tion: if we liquidate your life into a role in a farce or whatever, do you think
we've gotten all of it? Would we want to perform this liquidation, to fend off
unintelligibility this thoroughly? And why would we need to do that? Because
unintelligibility is a constant threat? Hardly, if human life is a quest narrative. But
by the same token, we are constantly threatened (or, in my case, comforted) by
unintelligibility, as MacIntyre's philosophy makes as clear as anyone's.

II

I suggested earlier that although seemingly unconnected, fragmentary, or
bizarre events can be swept up into narratives, even those narratives which display the sort of extreme coherence that MacIntyre requires can be swept back
into unintelligibility. I will consider here a figure whom MacIntyre makes central to modernity: Kierkegaard. Kierkegaard is central to MacIntyre because, in
Either/Or, Kierkegaard sets out a choice between the aesthetic and the ethical
as essentially arbitrary. (That is according to MacIntyre, and this much is right:
the choice is rationally arbitrary; no arguments will move one from the aesthetic to the ethical. But what moves one from the aesthetic to the ethical is
also not merely a whimsical preference; it is despair.) Thus, for MacIntyre,
Kierkegaard is symptomatic of the nightmare of modernity, in which rival
visions of life confront one another with no hope of rational resolution, a
nightmare that MacIntyre traces to the enlightenment conception of rationality as being value-neutral, and the post-enlightenment conception of values as
being emotive preferences.

The aesthetic life is, for Kierkegaard, the life that seeks to make itself interesting, that goes out and tries to sample the smorgasbord of experiences. It is
marked by a lack of seriousness. But the ethical, for Kierkegaard, orders life into
project, and demands the highest seriousness. This seriousness is encapsulated
according to *Either/Or* in the project of marriage as a lifetime commitment.
MacIntyre writes:

> When Kierkegaard contrasted the ethical and the aesthetic ways of
> life in *Enten/Eller*, he argued that the aesthetic life is one in which
> a human life is dissolved into a series of separate present moments,
> in which the unity of a human life disappears from view. By con-
> trast in the ethical life commitments and responsibilities to the
> future springing from past episodes in which obligations were con-
> ceived and debts assumed unite the present to past and future in
> such a way as to make of human life a unity. The unity to which
> Kierkegaard refers is [a] narrative unity. (241–42)

MacIntyre disagrees with Kierkegaard in the latter's account of the transition
from the aesthetic to the ethical. He also disagrees with Kierkegaard's account
of the ethical itself, which as MacIntyre points out is fundamentally Kantian.
But where MacIntyre agrees with (his own reading of) *Either/Or* is in the characterization of the ethical life as unified by narrative teleology in a way that the
aesthetic is not.

Two remarks: first, it is odd that Kierkegaard himself characterizes the aesthetic essentially through narrative; in setting out the aesthetic sphere, he calls
to his aid tales about Don Juan as well as many other tales. It is hard to imagine a more perfectly unified, teleologically-driven narrative than the "Diary of
a Seducer." Furthermore, when he comes to characterize the ethical with
regard to the life-project of marriage, Kierkegaard runs precisely into problems
with narrative. The narratives of love with which Judge William is familiar end
with marriage; it is the exciting and "interesting" events bound up with secur-
ing the beloved over a series of obstacles that form the narratives of love in
Western culture.

> Over the centuries have not knights and adventurers experienced
> incredible toil and trouble in order to find quiet peace in a happy
> marriage; over the centuries have not writers and readers of novels
> labored through one volume after another in order to end with a
> happy marriage; and has not one generation after the other again
> and again faithfully endured four acts of troubles and entanglements
> if only there was the probability of a happy marriage in the fifth act?
> But through these efforts very little is accomplished for the glorifi-
> cation of marriage, and I doubt very much that any person by read-
> ing such books has felt himself made competent to fulfill the task
> he has set for himself or has felt himself oriented in life, for precisely
> this is the corruption, the unhealthiness in these books, that they
> end where they should begin.[6]

---

6. *Either/Or*, trans. Howard V. Hong and Edna Hong (Princeton: Princeton University Press, 1987), vol. 2, p. 17.

The reason that there are not many narratives of long, happy marriages in which the parties involved find in marriage an ethical telos and devote their lives to its continuous realization is precisely that such a narrative would be insufficiently aesthetic. It would be boring, and Judge William's treatment of marriage is one of the most boring segments of Kierkegaard's entire oeuvre: it is pointedly boring, grindingly repetitive. The narrative of a happy marriage goes something like this: we committed ourselves to the project with utter seriousness, and then the next day we did the same, and the next day we did the same, and so on and on. Such a narrative is, in Aristotle's phrase, episodic. That is a funny thing about the ethical in relation to narrative: its successful realization consists fundamentally in episodes that embody that realization. In fact I don't think it is too much to say that by MacIntyre's standards there cannot be an ethical narrative on Kierkegaard's understanding of the ethical. For Kierkegaard, the ethical is that which has its telos in itself: the "purpose" of marriage is . . . itself. So a narrative of the ethical in Kierkegaard's sense isn't going anywhere; it is trying to find meaning and satisfaction in repetition. It is hard, however, to imagine a purely ethical narrative on any account of the ethical, though there can be narratives with an ethical upshot, which present barriers to the realization of the ethical, lapses away from it and recommitments to it. Thus, a decent narrative with ethical content is going to have to inscribe the failure of the ethical, its lapse, its rejection. Any decent narrative of the ethical is going to stand, that is, in excess to the ethical; it will show the ethical in a final victory, but it must also hold to the constant possibility of transgression. If the ethical is to be an achievement, then the transgression of the ethical is always going to be inscribed within it; *the ethical that is not threatened with collapse cannot be narrated.*

If we were in the mood to associate narrative and the ethical, we might also associate the foregoing insight with the insight that narratives themselves are always tenuous, that they take their character, among other things, from the character of what must be overcome in the achievement of the telos. And narrative is precisely the selection of material and its ordering into a whole that displays some degree of coherence and meaning; it is thus a safari into incoherence and meaninglessness, and part of the pleasure associated with narrative arises in building incoherences toward coherent closure.

P. G. Wodehouse is for my money a great master of narrative. And the structure of any Blandings Castle or Bertie and Jeeves adventure is this. We start with a simple idyllic situation, a lark, vacation, or interstice in the rush of life. One by one disturbing complications are introduced that push the situation to the brink of all-out madness. Then some genius in the cast—Galahad Threepwood or Jeeves—pulls a rabbit out of the hat and re-orders the chaos. All ends with perfect coherence and more or less for the best. The point in the plot that I want to emphasize is the moment of excruciating tension, when the complications have reached incredible intensity and resolution appears impossible. Without that moment, the Wodehousian narrative is inconceivable. And that moment is, of course, the moment of the highest comedy, the moment in which we are bewildered into laughter, the moment of ecstasy. The narrative is indeed an achievement of coherence, but the coherence would have no significance or value without the moment in which its possibility is submerged in the chaotic or rhizomatic intertwining of subplots. Each subplot is complicated exponentially and compromised in its coherence by its merging into the dense chaotic system whereby it is placed into relation with all the others. And of course Wodehouse's narratives, though they have an ethical undertow in their very innocence and lack of seriousness, are paradigmatically aesthetic. The usefulness of most characters to Wodehouse ends promptly at the moment of marriage, which is why Bertie and Galahad remain forever bachelors.

The value of narrative to life is made possible and given urgency by the chaotic moment, the moment of absurdity, incomprehension, intolerable complication. The form or organization is made possible and given its specific characteristics by a specific possibility or fact of a chaos. The Greek tragedy, for instance, arises as a possibility in the resolution of an ever-intensifying chaotic pain system into an inevitability. One shows that the incomprehensible or the bizarre could not have been otherwise, but to show that requires precisely a sojourn to the incomprehensible and bizarre. And this is a sojourn that we all take from time to time, though whether we will return to or arrive at the inevitable or the form of temporality is for us, as it is not for Bertie or Oedipus, an open question. And so we reach for narrative, strive for order as an achievement. This is paradoxical, for inevitability is precisely what cannot be achieved. That makes a problem of the relation of narrative to practical rationality, as we seek to impose upon ourselves a life that could not have been otherwise. A particular form of *amor fati*: fate as something we achieve. This paradox is revealed in the necessity attributed to practical rationality as the supposedly universal human condition; our will is supposed to be something we cannot escape. That is why there is supposed to be no temporality outside narrative; that is why narrative becomes a transcendental principle, a condition of possible experience. This should absolutely not be confused with a Nietzschean *amor fati*, which is precisely the realization that our fate cannot be achieved and that instrumental rationality is a hatred of life. Nietzsche's love of life is precisely a return into love as a chaotic system; better, it is itself a chaotic love.

The actual narrative resources available in the Western tradition for treat-
ing romantic love leave love at the moment that love is transformed from the
aesthetic to the ethical. It is worth noting that although MacIntyre treats narrative as essential to ethics, most of our narratives rollick through the aesthetic
in Kierkegaard's sense, for the aesthetic is entertaining and the ethical is boring.
(That is an aesthetic criticism of the ethical and of course does no damage to
the ethical considered on its own terms. It is Kierkegaard's point, in fact, that
neither the ethical nor the aesthetic can address or assess the other in its own
terms without begging the question. If my question is why I should bother living ethically, the only answer an advocate of the ethical can give me is an ethical answer: that is how you ought to live. If my question is how someone can
possibly live pre-ethically or aesthetically, the answer is that it is more interesting to live that way.) But that suggests at a minimum that MacIntyre's ethical
treatment of narrative is optional. In fact, many aspects of it are optional; narrative gets used for many different purposes in the contemporary discourse. For
example, MacIntyre places great weight on the singleness and coherence in
narratives that allow whole human lives to be made intelligible. But other
thinkers, including Rorty, emphasize precisely the multiplicity of alternative
narratives, as well as their ambiguity, in trying to show the centrality of narrative to human life. And if MacIntyre is caught up in ethical uses of narrative
(uses which in our culture at any rate are not the primary uses of narrative),
many others are more interested in the aesthetic uses, in the play of narrative,
and in narrative, and with narrative. If narrative can be used to suggest that our
fate can be achieved, it can also be used to show that our fate is a simplification of a chaos (Wodehouse) or that it is something in the face of which we
learn resignation or affirmation (Sophocles, Job, Nietzsche).

But what sets Kierkegaard most fundamentally in opposition to MacIntyre is not any of the points that MacIntyre selects for criticism, nor even his
misreading of those points with which he takes himself to be in sympathy. Mac-
Intyre omits Kierkegaard's treatment of the religious sphere in its entirety. Let
us remind ourselves of some of the fundamental tenets of Kierkegaard's account
of the religious. First of all, it goes through and then beyond the ethical: it pre-
supposes the ethical, but is "higher." Second, the religious is a movement made
by each individual one by one, not by committee. To perform one's social role
perfectly is what the ethical demands; the religious involves something that is
socially incomprehensible. To live ethically is to reconcile oneself to the universal or to seek to erase or expunge everything in oneself that is not perfectly
describable as universal. MacIntyre does not actually believe in "the universal"
in this sense, but we could put the point, in keeping with MacIntyre's concep-

tion of the ethical, by saying that the ethical demands the erasure of anything that is not perfectly articulated as the social, anything in the individual that has not been perfectly erased into what everyone inhabiting a given role can have in common. Of course, to say that there *is* in fact anything in anyone that exceeds the social is to beg the question against all these positions.

For Kierkegaard, if there is a place we are all driving toward, a telos we all share that makes sense of our lives, then history and God are "dilatory," they expend generation after generation; history or God should just cut to the chase, get it over with. The teleological in MacIntyre's sense and the religious in Kierkegaard's are perfectly incommensurable, because in the teleological order individual human beings are their social functions, so much so that the individual human being ought in all conscience to be omitted from the social entirely. And there is not enough intrinsic information of the world-historical process; it is too teleologically driven—so teleologically driven that the process itself ought in all good conscience to be omitted entirely.

> If one posits only the evolution of the race, the generations of men, how does one explain the divine wastefulness which uses the infinite host of individuals one generation after the other merely for the purpose of setting the world-historical process going? The world-historical drama is infinitely dilatory: why does not God hasten, if that is all He wants? What an undramatic exhibition of patience, or, rather, what a prosaic and tiresome procrastination! . . . But if the task of becoming subjective is the highest that is proposed to a human being, everything is beautifully arranged. First it follows that world-history is no concern of his, but that everything in this connection is to be left to the royal poet. In the next place there is no waste of human lives; for even if individuals were as numberless as the sands of the sea, the task of becoming subjective is given to each.[7]

For Kierkegaard we are all inevitably and continually subjects. And becoming subjective is becoming apparent before God, for whom all things are already apparent. Thus the highest human task or project is becoming what one already is.

> It is commonly assumed that no art or skill is required in order to be subjective. To be sure, every human being is a bit of a subject, in a sense. But now to strive to become what one already is: who would take the pains to waste his time on such a task, involving the greatest possible degree of resignation? Quite so. But for this very

---

7. Kierkegaard, *Concluding Unscientific Postscript*, trans. David Swenson and Walter Lowrie (Princeton: Princeton University Press, 1968), pp. 141–42.

> reason alone it is a very difficult task, the most difficult of all tasks
> in fact, precisely because every human being has a strong natural
> bent and passion to become something more and different. (116)

Now let me hang a few remarks on these bewildering passages. First of all, the ethical (as it is conceived in *Either/Or* and not as it is conceived in the *Postscript*)—the universal, the world-historical, or the social—is, if it is conceived as the highest, a "tiresome and prosaic procrastination." It is best left to the most prosaic possible poet: the court poet. The species or the culture as a project is both delusional and boring, unworthy of the intensity that makes a true poetry, or rather, impossible to advocate or describe with any intensity at all, because that intensity would be jagged to the social, would appear to be an assertion of particularity and so either impossible or sinful by its own account. But the poetry of intense passion itself could be thought of as narratively and teleologically organized; the telos is, however, what you already are. Your goal is to end up exactly where you are without moving, or to become with ever more intensity what you can never cease to be with total intensity. This will involve a narrative that is circular or that is a sheer repetition: a narrative of the becoming-apparent before God of what never ceases to be perfectly apparent to God. And that, in turn, is going to require in the religious sphere the reduction of the teleology of Aristotle and MacIntyre to absurdity; Kierkegaard pledges to show us the comedy in the seriousness with which we devote ourselves to goals external to ourselves, by which we become "world-historical entrepreneurs" or "world-historical swashbucklers." And the comedy is devastating: it involves taking questions that are fairly simple when objectively considered (questions like: what does it mean to die?) and showing that they land us in infinite complications as soon as they are treated subjectively. But then none of us ever ceased to be a subject, or ceased to face death as a subject. As in Wodehouse, the moment of intolerable complication and redundancy and self-referentiality becomes the moment of comedic artistry.

Most significantly for present purposes, the religious, the movement of faith, is a movement out of meaning entirely as meaning is humanly or socially constructed. Faith for Kierkegaard is an absurdity, a paradox that is believed with total commitment. It cannot even be stated without appearing idiotic or impossible. There is thus, for Kierkegaard, an aesthetic moment before one orders one's entire life with deep seriousness into a coherent project; this moment lies before the ethical, though it makes rich use of narrative. There is then the ethical itself, in which one finds, MacIntyre-like, one's meaning in a teleologically driven project that suffices for one's life. And then there is a moment in which this project is both preserved and destroyed, in which one lurches into the incomprehensible.

Perhaps Kierkegaard's most deeply moving statement of the religious is found in his treatment of the Abraham and Isaac story in *Fear and Trembling*. Notice that this statement emerges precisely out of a story; Kierkegaard is, in a parody of preachers through the centuries, using the narrative of Abraham and Isaac as a parable of faith. What I want to point out is what this does for my side of the standoff. Kierkegaard uses this story precisely to show us a way beyond stories; for Kierkegaard, the narrative of Abraham and Isaac shows a "parable of faith," a little narrative lesson on faith as a virtue and a life-project, to be the deepest betrayal of faith. When Kierkegaard locates the central unintelligibility of this story, he uses the narrative to reach beyond the possibility of narrative and of the ethical as MacIntyre conceives them.

Alright then: God demands that Abraham sacrifice his beloved son as a test of his faith. Then at the last minute God withdraws Isaac from the sacrifice and substitutes a ram. But Abraham is willing to do what God demands. Kierkegaard ridicules the preachers who simply say that Abraham was willing to give God the best he had, and leave it at that. He imagines a parishioner hearing such a sermon and going home on Sunday afternoon, eating dinner, and then killing his own son, so as to give God the best he has. The preacher would be horrified and condemn such a one as a murderer and would certainly say that he had misunderstood the sermon. And yet what can the story of Abraham possibly mean?

For Kierkegaard, what is missing in the sermon is precisely the movement of faith by which Abraham, while continuing to recognize the absolute moral obligation that he is under to preserve and nurture his son, leaves the universal ethical obligation behind and becomes willing to commit the most monstrous crime. "The ethical expression for what Abraham did was that he was willing to commit murder."[8] God is himself the source of the ethical prohibitions that he demands that Abraham suspend, and one might almost say that God is in the story a murderer as well as the lawgiver who prohibits murder. But all of this is perfectly absurd, contradictory, unintelligible. What God demands of Abraham, finally, is the utter destruction of his practical rationality, the utter destruction of his narratives. What is omitted in the sermon is the anguish, as for three days, Abraham travels to the mountain where he is to sacrifice Isaac, as he gazes moment by moment at the person he loves most in the

---

8. *Fear and Trembling*, trans. Alastair Hannay (New York: Penguin, 1985 [1843]), p. 60.

world, as he holds on moment by moment to the knowledge that what he is about to do is a monstrous crime, as he holds also moment by moment to the resolution to do it anyway, decides again at each moment to obey God's will, which is internally contradictory.

> Abraham cannot be mediated, which can also be put by saying that he cannot speak. The moment I speak I express the universal, and when I do not no one can understand me. So the moment Abraham wants to express himself in the universal, he has to say that his situation is one of temptation, for he has no higher expression of the universal that overrides the universal he transgresses. (89)

Later, Kierkegaard adds:

> Thus what could Abraham have done? If he had wanted to say to someone: "I love Isaac more than everything in the world, and that's why it's so hard for me to sacrifice him," the person would surely have shaken his head and said: "Then why sacrifice him?".... Faith is this paradox, that the single individual is quite unable to make himself intelligible to anyone. (98, 99)

God thus calls Abraham to a transgression that is shattering, a transgression that shatters his relation to the ethical, shatters his social role, shatters his intelligibility. And the central point for present purposes is that Kierkegaard moves us by narrative into unintelligibility, just as the movement into the religious is made by means of the ethical and preserves the ethical. For if one did not also recognize the binding force of the ethical obligation, one could not come to reside in the paradox when one wills the violation of that obligation. The ethical must be recognized in its universally binding force, and it must be transgressed. And the Abraham story must be taken as a parable of faith, but of a faith that shatters the narrative construction of a human life.

Recall that MacIntyre identifies human lives with social roles; for MacIntyre, there is no subject aside from the roles one discharges. This is to bring the individual wholly into the realm of what Kierkegaard calls the universal or the ethical or the intelligible. MacIntyre wants above all to make us intelligible to one another, to impose or reimpose intelligibility and to lop off whatever exceeds or rejects the intelligible. Now MacIntyre does not think of moral rules as universal; rather, he thinks of social roles as emerging in practices and articulating a human telos from within those practices. However, to treat people as merely the roles they perform seems to be a bureaucratic vision of the self of exactly the sort that MacIntyre deplores; it would follow from MacIntyre's view, for example, that anyone could be perfectly replaced, if someone could be found who performed the same roles. In fact, if human selfhood is a role in a drama of whatever genre our lives are instantiating at the moment, someone else could actually become me by taking up my roles.

On Kierkegaard's use of the Abraham story, God confronts Abraham utterly as a single individual; he strips Abraham of his "role" as a father, with all its ethical/narrative accessories.

> The ethical as such is the universal, and as the universal it applies to everyone, which can be put from another point of view by saying it applies at every moment. . . . Seen as an immediate, no more than sensate and psychic, being, the single individual is the particular that has its telos in the universal, and the individual's ethical task is always to express himself in this, to abrogate his particularity so as to become the universal. As soon as the single individual wants to assert himself in his particularity, in direct opposition to the universal, he sins, and only by recognizing this can he again reconcile himself with the universal. . . . If that is the case, then Hegel is right in his "Good and Conscience" where he discusses man seen merely as the single individual and regards this way of seeing him as a "moral form of evil" to be annulled in the teleology of the ethical life. . . . Where Hegel goes wrong, on the other hand, is in talking about faith, in not protesting loudly and clearly against the honour and glory paid to Abraham as the father of faith when he should really be remitted to some lower court for trial and exposed as a murderer.
>
> For faith is just this paradox, that the single individual is higher than the universal. (83–84)

Now I suspect that, just as he terms a single human action an abstraction from a narrative, MacIntyre might treat human individuals as abstractions from their social roles rather than vice versa. But the point here is that for MacIntyre there is no place at all beyond or before or above what Kierkegaard terms the universal. There is, to put it another way, no place for sin understood as the assertion or realization of particularity, no sense of the centrality precisely for narrative of the node of the narrative in which the ethical or the social is lost, transgressed, compromised. As Kierkegaard's Hegel prescribes becoming-universal, sees all history and life as a merging into identity with the universal, MacIntyre prescribes becoming social, or holds that we are always already without remainder of the social order. In either case, an assertion of particularity, whether it is an assertion of selfhood in distinction to social role, an assertion of the importance of the present moment, an assertion of faith, or whatever, must be sin. And such an assertion would be, for MacIntyre, incomprehensible or self-contradictory; it would declare the self to be what no self can be; it would declare autonomy of the moment from a narrative ordering; it would declare the value of a transgression of values. And yet we are all familiar with such moments, the value of which is not least that they draw us away from the busy narrative absence in which we enshroud ourselves and call us into the places where, gloriously or shatteringly, meanings break down or exceed our capacities, the places where we let go of meaning.

Now Abraham's movement into faith, or display of his already-existing faith, is accomplished precisely by a transgression of the ethical. For Kierkegaard, it is this transgression which breaks the narrative into absurdity and hence opens the story to faith. But notice that no such moment is possible on MacIntyre's treatment of human life as a coherent, teleologically driven narrative project. The feeling that one has in the midst of an ethical transgression or a religious experience is precisely the feeling of letting go of the account one has given to oneself of oneself; one is finding out that one is capable of things which lie outside the narrative one has made for oneself. This is certainly true if narratives are ethically driven, as MacIntyre believes, or if ethics is narratively driven. Just as the resolution or seduction to transgression is what breaks the narrative of the Abraham story, so seductions into evil are what break our stories about ourselves. And the story itself is impossible without the story being broken, just as the breaking of the story is impossible without the story itself and its resolution. There is no possibility of narrative unless the narrative form is somewhere disarticulated, just as that disarticulation is performed on the very thread out of which the narrative web is spun.

If we conceive life as an ethical project, as a quest, then it is no wonder that evil appears in the form of narrative incoherence and that narrative incoherence itself appears as an explosion of particularity. (The complications in a Wodehouse plot introduce the crazy profusion of particularities into the instrumental process by which the characters are reconciled to the universal [marriage] and thus achieve their fate in a role.) And it is really no wonder that we want to be seduced into evil, for to live one's every waking moment in pursuit of some goal is a very protestant form of inquisition. For that reason, since we are oppressed by our projects and trapped in our roles, moments of transgression are, precisely, moments of ecstasy.

MacIntyre might say that our sense of entrapment is itself a mark of bourgeois individualism; we fancy ourselves to be selves that stand outside our socially articulated roles and hence feel ourselves constrained. And the fact that our culture has become a welter of competing visions of the good allows us to feel that we could float freely among them, that it is up to ourselves to construct our narratives. But our entrapment is, I fear, much more a result of the pervasiveness in our culture of views such as MacIntyre's, views that demand of each person a life lived in the service of a project, which bring to bear the gigantic machinery of productivity, of the self conceived technologically. Unless one can simply eradicate massive zones of oneself, including various bodily recalcitrances and so forth, I really do not see how such a life could fail to be experienced at times as an oppression. And of course, if one sets about eradicating the recalcitrant zones, one is in a hopeless project of self-mutilation.

That raises an issue I would like to pursue briefly: that our power to make ourselves over is limited, supposing it exists at all. I cannot make myself ethical by insisting that I be ethical, or by telling myself at all times what to do (as in, on a certain interpretation, Aristotle's practical syllogism). That strategy simply makes transgression an obsession, and will quickly convert me into a monster. If I am experiencing the universalizing or ethical narrative of my life—my social roles—as an oppression, there is no question of simply forcing myself into a productive mode. For MacIntyre believes, I think, that reinstituting coherent narratives of human lives will reshape those lives; indeed, he can hardly believe otherwise, since he identifies lives and narratives. But reinstituting (if ever, indeed, there were) coherent narratives at this point would simply increase the distance between narratives and lives. We can go ahead and deny that this distance exists, but to deny that people experience this distance, whether or not they are hallucinating, would obviously be to assert a falsehood.

Kierkegaard, on the other hand, proposes a paradoxical teleology in which the goal is to become what we already are, but now in deep appreciation or complete immersion. By being willing to commit the transgression, to break his narrative apart utterly, Abraham receives Isaac back; Abraham's faith enables him to do God's will where God wills the transgression and that enables him to receive Isaac again. The whole exercise appears from one point of view to be absolutely pointless: Abraham ends in one sense precisely where he began; as a loving father and a man of faith; he receives nothing that he did not already have; his narrative is reinstituted and indeed it was never compromised, for Abraham held on to the ethical, to God's law, even in his resolution to violate it. He resigned his practical rationality utterly even while he held on to it completely. So the narrative, even conceived in its entirety, surveyed whole, is incommensurable, utterly incommensurable, with the order of teleology. It represents a prodigious, a superhuman degree of moral and religious strength, all of it devoted to the end of achieving what is already the case. But that is precisely how Kierkegaard refuses to treat the narrative; he refuses to survey it as a whole, to "skip to the end," where Abraham receives Isaac back, because that is precisely to skip over Abraham's greatness: the ethical which is simultaneously held and transgressed, that is, "suspended," and the anguish, the existential situation in which Abraham finds himself at every moment:

> But it is the outcome that arouses our curiosity, as with the con-
> clusion of a book; one wants nothing of the fear, the distress, the
> paradox. One flirts with the outcome aesthetically; it comes as
> unexpectedly and yet as effortlessly as a prize in a lottery; and hav-
> ing heard the outcome one is improved. And yet no robber of tem-
> ples hard-labouring in chains is so base a criminal as he who plun-
> ders the holy in this way, and not even Judas, who sold his master
> for thirty pieces of silver, is more contemptible than the person who
> would thus offer greatness for sale. (92)

Abraham is great in virtue of his beginning upon the journey, not in virtue of his receiving Isaac back; he is great in resigning himself to losing Isaac while still believing that he will receive Isaac again. And he is great in the fact that his end is his beginning, that in the journey he does not actually get anywhere, that he achieves what he is.

In entering the eternal Abraham receives the temporal, in which he has never ceased to have his life and his existence; in a transgression of teleology he has received again his telos, to which he has never ceased to be fully committed.

> Faith is therefore no aesthetic emotion, but something far higher,
> exactly because it presupposes resignation; it is not the immediate
> inclination of the heart but the paradox of existence. . . . I can see
> that it requires strength and energy and freedom of the spirit to
> make the infinite movement of resignation; I can also see that it can
> be done. The next step dumbfounds me, my brain reels; for having
> made the movement of resignation, now on the strength of the
> absurd to get everything, to get one's desire, whole, in full, that
> requires more-than-human powers. (76)

Abraham achieves his telos by giving up his telos. And his telos is precisely to become again what he never ceased to be: a man of resignation and of hope, Isaac's father. This is, for Kierkegaard, precisely a narrative of what it makes no sense whatever to narrate, a narrative of letting go of narrative.

Kierkegarard famously describes two knights: the knight of infinite resignation and the knight of faith. The knight of infinite resignation submits him-
self utterly to God's will and does not make the mistake of thinking that this will is going to be comprehensible in terms of human practical rationality. He is ready for the transgression; his narrative is shattered. He is the spiritual hero or the man of extraordinary spirituality: the monk who devotes his life to God and for whom life is changed utterly by this devotion because he knows that God's

will is incomprehensible. The metaphor that Kierkegaard draws is to a middle class boy who falls in love with a princess, realizes with perfect clarity that he can never have her, and yet resolves to find the only meaning of his life in his love, holds to his hopeless and irrational love at every moment as his deepest commitment. Now that is an odd teleology, where I am absolutely committed to realizing a telos that I am all along certain can never be achieved. At that point, teleology and practical rationality are detached from one another; there is nothing I can do to realize the telos by my own lights and so I resign myself completely to the fact that my life is, in a certain sense, futile. And yet I also hold to that telos—perhaps even to that futility—as the ultimate meaning of my life.

That is a noble kind of life, according to Kierkegaard, though one that it is almost impossible to choose. But it is still not the highest sort of life or spirituality: the life of the knight of faith. In the metaphor, the knight of faith does exactly what the knight of infinite resignation does: he realizes or believes that he will never get the princess, and yet he knows that he will get her anyway, because for God all things are possible. Now that gets you into an even worse position with regard to practical rationality, because you believe both that the telos is impossible of achievement—that there is nothing you can do to achieve it—and that it will be achieved anyway. The knight of faith renounces the temporal in favor of the eternal and receives thereby precisely the temporal. In one of the most beautiful and bizarre assertions in the history of philosophy, Kierkegaard asserts that the knight of faith is absolutely indistinguishable from the tax collector; he's just a solid guy who is fully committed to the temporal. He is as embedded in the order of human teleology as it is possible to be; no hint of the eternal gleams from his eyes. His commitment to the eternal *is* his reception of the temporal; Abraham's perfect reconciliation to God's incomprehensible will *is* his reception again of Isaac and his taking up again of his social role.

Thus the knight of infinite resignation becomes something extraordinary; he overcomes the teleological order and becomes a kind of spiritual exemplar. But the knight of faith becomes nothing; he becomes only what he already is. And here the order of teleology is both completely present or reinstated and absolutely transcended: if my "goal" were actually to become exactly what I already am, how would I "organize" my life in order to achieve that goal? Rather, I would simply *let go*. Any moment of letting go is in some sense or to some degree an abrogation of the teleological order, but the moment of letting go into what one already is, the moment where the tax-collector lets go precisely into being a tax-collector, is a moment in which the teleological order is shattered precisely by and in its own perfect presence.

CHAPTER TWO

SIGN AND SIN

I

MacIntyre's view is extreme. One aspect of this extremity is found in his account of narrative, which appears to have very little play and to impose extreme criterial requirements of coherence and meaningfulness. I will now take up a somewhat milder and more nuanced account of narrative—that of Paul Ricoeur—and try to show that many of the same problems arise in Ricoeur's treatment. New problems also arise, in particular regarding issues of time and history. Ricoeur formulates the following fundamental principle:

> [B]etween the activity of narrating a story and the temporal character of human experience there exists a correlation that is not merely accidental but that presents a transcultural form of necessity. To put it another way, time becomes human to the extent that it is articulated through a narrative mode, and narrative attains its full meaning when it becomes a condition of temporal existence.[1]

This formulation is somewhat ambiguous, though the ambiguity is productive for Ricoeur. For it may mean that human beings can only experience time in narrative, or it may mean that time, itself inhuman, is humanized in being narrated. And the formulation he provides toward the end of *Time and Narrative* is

---

1. *Time and Narrative*, vol. 1, trans. Kathleen McLaughlin and David Pellauer (Chicago: University of Chicago Press, 1984), p. 52.

ambiguous in the same way: "temporality . . . requires the mediation of the indirect discourse of narration. . . . There can be no thought about time without narrated time."[2]

The notion that narrative becomes a condition of temporal existence, or that temporality requires the mediation of narrative, hints that there is temporal existence or temporality which is not yet conditioned or mediated by narrative. But such an "unconditioned" time would be, for Ricoeur, inhuman, which suggests, among other things, that it would be incomprehensible. Human time is thus comprehensible time, that is, time that can be grasped and utilized in a variety of ways. Time "in itself," unconditioned by narrative, is prehuman time, something that we have always already left behind insofar as we are human. Ricoeur is, then, committed to the principle that human experience of time is always an experience of narration. This is suggested by the fact that, unlike MacIntyre, he explicitly grounds narrativism in a hermeneutic textualism of the sort we surveyed in the introduction: "If, in fact, human action can be narrated, it is because it is always already articulated by signs, rules, and norms. It is always already symbolically mediated" (57). Alternately: "language is the great institution, the institution of institutions, that has preceded each and every one of us" (vol. 3, 221). Now the initially quoted principle refers to human experience, while this last passage refers to human action as the material of narrative, which presages Ricoeur's treatment of issues in historiography. And it is worth remarking on the humanist presumptions here: first, that human action is what fundamentally gets narrated, and second, that "human experience" takes place in the "human time" of narrative. Of course, and as Ricoeur is well aware, human action takes place under ubiquitous material and nonhuman constraints, and human experience is in large measure an experience precisely of such constraints.[3] But such constraints can themselves be "humanized" by being taken up by narrative into "human time." That is, such constraints constitute barriers to practical rationality which make such rationality necessary. They are both the conditions that require instrumentalities so that the conditions themselves can be overcome, and also the conditions that are transformed into instrumentalities, as when some recalcitrant material is transformed into a

---

2. *Time and Narrative* vol. 3, trans. Kathleen Blamey and David Pellauer (Chicago: University of Chicago Press: 1988).

3. That he is aware of that becomes at least fairly obvious by the third volume of *Time and Narrative*. See in particular 261 ff. At times I think that Ricoeur is an amazingly balanced thinker. At others I think he simply takes back precisely what he asserts most emphatically.

tool. Further, they are conditions that yield the possibility and form of the instrumentalities we can achieve; the form and use of the pliers is in part articulated by the recalcitrance of the metal out of which it is made, and the recalcitrance of metal is precisely what pliers are used to overcome or address.

The quick transition from experience to action is, however, problematic. Ricoeur, like MacIntyre, gives an Aristotelian account of action as organized teleologically, which immediately (for contemporary ears, at any rate) suggests narration. However, it is far from obvious that experience is organized teleologically. Experience seems to be something that happens to us, and though one might always act for ends (though for the record I don't think so), it seems odd to experience for ends. Of course, one might go out and cultivate experiences that relate to one's life-goals; that is possible. And of course, one might hold (as Gadamer and many others have held) that experience itself is always already symbolically mediated, that our signs have already performed the effaced work of making our experience possible to ourselves or of making an experiencable world. But imagine, for a moment, experience conceived through and through teleologically, or imagine an experiencable world that displayed no excess to symbol systems. I'm going to start railing about this in a bit, but let me say: life in such a world is redundant; all you're doing is traversing what has always already been traversed, finding what you yourself and the other munchkins of the sign put there in the first place. It's fun to hide something from someone else, but hiding something from yourself is not a very diverting game.

At any rate, like MacIntyre, Ricoeur presents us with an Aristotelian account of human action, one that is teleologically driven. "Actions imply goals," he writes (55). To order action by narrative is (in part) to say what it is *for*, where it is leading. This is an element of what Ricoeur terms "emplotment," which is the rendering of action or experience into a coherent form, a form that displays character, telos, and topic.

> To explain why something happened and to describe what happened coincide. A narrative that fails to explain is less than a narrative. A narrative that does explain is a pure, plain narrative. (148)

It would follow from this, for Ricoeur, that all events in time (or human time) are explicable, and that insofar as they are experienced in human time have already been explained (which is assuredly not to say that they have been explained once and for all, that they cannot be renarrated). The narrative explains; but the narrative gives you the action or the experience in the first place, makes it in the first place possible, or is itself the action or experience.

That is why I suggested that life for the munchkin of the sign is redundant; our fundamental activity is explaining what comes ready-explained, or what cannot but be explained in virtue of its sheer occurrence.

This is, of course, bound up with narrative teleology.

> To follow a story, in effect, is to understand the successive actions, thoughts, and feelings in the story inasmuch as they present a particular "directedness." Let us understand by this that we are "pulled forward" by the development, as soon as we respond with expectations concerning the completion and outcome of the whole process. (150)

We need to keep in mind that, if Ricoeur is right, it would follow that such remarks could be extended to any event in time. That is, in human time, every event is always tending somewhere; anything that takes up a place in time, that finds a place in time, always already displays a particular "directedness." This would be strange enough. But now consider for a moment the directedness of "feelings." Someone you love just died: you are bereft. Whereto your bereftness? What is it for? Every response to this question which does not simply dismiss or attack the question is an obscenity.

And as in Aristotle and MacIntyre, it is only on such a teleological basis that, for Ricoeur, actions can be ascribed moral content. Their directedness, their existence in the dimension of practical rationality, renders them explicable, and the explication is going to have an ethical upshot precisely because the action is rationally directed. There appears to be, in Ricoeur, no human action and no moment of human experience that is not held in the sway of the ethical.

> If tragedy can represent [characters] as "better" and comedy as "worse" than actual human beings, it is because the practical understanding authors share with their audiences necessarily involves an evaluation of the characters and their actions in terms of good and bad. There is no action that does not give rise to approbation or reprobation, to however small a degree, as a function of a hierarchy of values for which goodness and wickedness are the poles. . . . [P]oetics does not stop borrowing from ethics, even when it advocates the suspension of all ethical judgment or its ironic inversion. The very project of ethical neutrality presupposes the original ethical quality of action on the prior side of fiction. This ethical quality is itself only a corollary of the major characteristic of action, that it is always symbolically mediated. (59)

Thus, for Ricoeur, the ethical is held within the very possibility of the symbolic. That we are capable of experiencing anything at all, which requires that

our experience be always already symbolically mediated, inscribes this experience, every single bit of it, always already within the ethical. There is no escape
from the ethical, no surcease, unless this escape is also an escape from experience and action. (Hayden White has argued compellingly that narrative history
emerges only in and as a moral/political order of significance, a thought that I
will end up exploring at some length.[4]) The above passage is a bit odd because
it actually seems confused as between whether it is doing literary criticism or
world criticism; it is actually not clear whether Ricoeur is referring to characters in tragedies and comedies, or to all of us, the munchkins of the sign. But
this is what we should expect, I guess: finally an actual confusion about whether
we are fictional or factual, whether I'm an animal body, or rather just play one
on television.

Just as does MacIntyre, Ricoeur makes the concept of individual or collective identity turn on narration:

> To state the identity of an individual or a community is to answer
> the question "Who did this?" "Who is the agent, the author?" We
> first answer this question by naming someone, that is, by designat-
> ing them with a proper name. But what is the basis for the per-
> manence of this proper name? What justifies our taking the subject
> of an action, so designated by his, her, or its proper name, as the
> same throughout a life that stretches from birth to death? The
> answer has to be narrative. . . . [L]ife itself [is] a cloth woven of sto-
> ries told. (vol 3, 246)

Now this would mean, for example, that if my life ceases to have a coherent
plot, if its sense begins to collapse, if I lose the thread of the story I was telling
or others lose the thread of the story they were telling about me, if no one can
make sense of my life (and in all the aspects in which my life already fails to
make sense), then there is no me. It is impossible, literally senseless, to say of
some person that their story has broken down or that their life displays a lapse
in narrative coherence. At that point you're talking about several people inhabiting the same body, though I suppose the identity of bodies itself would be a
narrative notion, so that if your story breaks down your body disappears and
perhaps another one virtually indistinguishable from the first arrives to occupy
the same bit of space. So we must always hold every human self to high standards of coherence (though, it is important to note, not as high as the standards
MacIntyre would impose, for reasons we will see) or watch it cease to be itself.

---

4. E.g., Hayden White, *The Content of the Form* (Baltimore: Johns Hopkins University Press, 1987), p. 14.

Since human time is a time of character, topic, and telos, a time of narrative and thus a coherent time, it is always subject to ethical evaluation; indeed, Ricoeur, in what is perhaps a slip of the pen, seems to assert that there is no human action which escapes ethical evaluation. And these claims, which despite Ricoeur's magisterial composure are, to say the least, controversial, follow directly from his account, not of God, or the Good, but of time in relation to narrative and practical rationality.

Think seriously for a minute about what you do and what you experience in a day. Better, think about the richness contained in a single glance. Then think, first, about the impoverished character of any human sign system with regard to the content of any glance: how far we are from being able to describe it, how far we are from wanting to, how far we are from needing to. Look at a wall, and think seriously for a moment what would be involved in attempting to squeeze that experience, all of it, into the order of the sign; now add the other sense modalities and their contents; now add the feelings within your body. Now think about the act you are performing: intentionally looking at a wall, in fact, looking at it for certain ends. Now try to rank that experience on a hierarchy of values. Even if something comes to mind here, think about whether you usually do that with glances at a wall, think about whether you want to do that with all such glances and whether you could. Think seriously about the torturous obsession that would ensue from taking that approach to life. And then think seriously about what it is that Ricoeur is actually proposing as an account of human action and experience and identity. It's not that Ricoeur's wrong; it's that he's obviously wrong, and that if we are to live tolerable lives, we must absolutely require his wrongness.

One thing about human time: it's a hell of a place for human beings to be. Life in human time is a life lived among the signs, life as a genre study, life as a publication, life as a CV. Now of course what I hate about the hectoring voice in me that identifies my life and my career is that it manifests a self-division. My will drags forward a tired body; the body falls into temptation conceived as a letting-go of the sign. Signlessness is the condition of sin. But a phenomenology of self-division, of the division of sign and sin, will and body, human time and time, cannot arise on Ricoeur's view. He simply sweeps sin, body, time into the patriarchy of the sign from the outset (though, as I said earlier, he seems by the end to want to have it both ways, which is what I think is meant by the word *hermeneutics*). Such a division of the self must then be an illusion; there is not the event and then the narration of the event, or the self and the narration of the self; the event and the self are constituted (and here that means produced without remainder) in their narration.

Consider the following passage from Deleuze and Guattari:

> There is always an appeal to a dominant reality that functions from
> within (already in the Old Testament, and during the Reforma-
> tion, with trade and capitalism). There is no longer even a need for
> a transcendent center of power; power is instead immanent and
> melds with the "real," operating through normalization. A strange
> invention: as if in one form the doubled subject were the cause of
> the statement of which, in its other form, it is itself a part. This is
> the paradox of the legislator-subject replacing the signifying
> despot: the more you obey the statements of the dominant reality,
> the more in command you are as subject of enunciation in mental
> reality, for in the end you are only obeying yourself! You are the
> one in command, in your capacity as a rational being. A new form
> of slavery is invented, namely being a slave to oneself, or to pure
> "reason," the Cogito.[5]

This passage begins to bring to bear the political critique of textualism and narrativism that I will explore at length later. When the world and the self are collapsed into the order of the sign as a condition of possible experience, the political power that is exercised through the sign, and which inheres in the character
of the sign, is simultaneously activated and concealed; it is activated by its concealment. That human subjects are zones of inscription for particular
sign/power configurations, particular economic contexts and institutions that
cannot operate without texts, is concealed as a metaphysics and ethics of human
being-in-the-world, so that even very particular inscriptions (such as that of
practical rationality) and very particular uses of such inscriptions (such as a
technological conception of the human relation to nature) are "naturalized" or
rather metaphysicalized (sorry) into basic conditions of human existence, or
into basic configurations of the "human" world. Indeed, the "humanization" of
the world, the collapse of the separation between, say, time "as it is" and time
"as it is experienced" is a reification of power relations, here conceived most
generally as the power of human beings over "our" universe. This relation is in
turn serviceable in particular regimes.

To take the sign and the narrative and their rationality to be the structure of human action and experience, to achieve the complete a priori normalization of the human subject as a condition of any possible experience, is
to seek a reunification of the doubled subject. One reconciles oneself to the
power that reinscribes one's body in regimes of significance by identifying

---

5. Gilles Deleuze and Felix Guattari, *A Thousand Plateaus*, trans. Brian Massumi
(Minneapolis: University of Minnesota Press, 1987), pp. 129–30.

those inscriptions with oneself, by dehistoricizing and deoptionalizing them. Now both MacIntyre and Ricoeur are "historicists"; they see ethics emerging through time in the unfolding of narratives. Yet they are antihistoricists in prescribing a general strategy for human normalization, or rather in saying that this normalization has always already been successfully performed, that human beings are roles, for example. MacIntyre's strategy for ethically empowering the self is a smooth reconciliation with some system of signs or narratives, never mind (for now) which. He acknowledges that different cultures and different eras have different rationalities; only he insists that every culture has something that he will recognize as a rationality, a position that is also held by Habermas. There is a wave in the direction of difference, strangeness, transgression and so on; then there is the reappropriation of all difference into the rationality of the author: the Western practical rationality that owes its earliest formulation to Aristotle. We'll let you do your thing, only you've got to make yourselves intelligible to us, and of course you can too, because our rationality, our narrative is the transcendental ground of human experience. But it might be pointed out that the textualizing of human experience and action, and the textualizing of the "human world" are disciplinary artifacts, that one is rendered a textual subject by being subjected to texts. To accept this rendering is to empower oneself precisely within the regime of signs by which one is subjected by becoming a node of that very regime. One can then be borne aloft by the sign and participate in the work of subjecting other people to it. One renders oneself a single, coherent subject by speaking the words that are always already being spoken to one, in one, at one. One causes the statement of which one is already a part.

To take the role, sign, narrative as the always already is to seek to render invisible the structures that articulate subjectivities in disciplines bound up with sign systems. It is to assert that, finally, any tension or schizophrenia experienced in the face of the normalization by signs is based on some sort of confusion, for one's experience is bleat under the order of the sign from the outset. That MacIntyre, say, expunges lives into roles is, then, less than no surprise; he seeks to render one's enrollment in some regime of signs a transcendental category.

According to Deleuze and Guattari, the normalizing machine of significance that is bound to Western conceptions of reason puts every person in command of themselves insofar as they are representatives of that machine, or rather locations within it. Thus, the more effortlessly one liquidates oneself into the regime of Western rationality, the more "autonomous" one is, the freer one is (consider Kant). This makes comprehensible the centrality of narrative (of certain narratives) to Western ethics. The freedom of the individual subject is proportional to the perfect liquidation of the subject into its roles, that is, into a narrative regime.

The choice that faces us, then, is not a choice between human freedom and knuckling under to the regime of signs. On the contrary, freedom in our tradition is conceived to be precisely this knuckling under. The choice is not between subjectivity and role. On the contrary, autonomous subjectivity is manufactured by power/sign configurations. By making narrative into a transcendental category, one short-circuits the possibility of zones of resistance, of internal divisions, forms of recalcitrance, flight to other sign systems, minor languages, subcultures, and so on. That is why MacIntyre bemoans modernity, because he conceives of it as a breakdown of the forms of dominance inscribed in master narratives.

Now if there is anything that we ought to have learned from deconstruction, it is this: that we should always get suspicious when a dualism is deployed and one of its terms seems to be effortlessly or unquestioningly or obviously privileged. We must look at that point for the covert dependence of the privileged term on its underprivileged shadow and show this, as a way to display the fact that the terms only make sense in their mutual simultaneous articulation. Here again we arrive at a treatment of what I called earlier a standoff. When MacIntyre or Ricoeur or many other textualists and narrativists arrive at this standoff, they run out of arguments completely and rest content with bald assertions. I think this is for the very good reason that there are no arguments here (on either side, by the way) that are not more or less obviously tendentious and question-begging. (There are, however, genealogies, causes for suspicion, strategies for creating suspicion.) The only way we could show that time was narrative all the way down, or that experience was always already symbolically mediated, would be to deduce this from itself. Suppose it were true that experience is always symbolically mediated. Then we could not show that it was, because as munchkins of the sign there's no vantage point from which to get a glimpse of the whole situation. We're always located in some zone of the sign inescapably; we're not tall enough to get hold of the whole human situation. Suppose on the other hand that experience is radically in excess to the sign. Then we couldn't show this except in signs, except by making signs to indicate what is supposed to be in excess to the sign. In short, no argument does any good either way.

Now it is certainly the case that, in recommending ethical neutrality or, as in Kierkegaard, describing ethical transgression, one inscribes the very ethical values that one rejects, one's rejection is incoherent without the prior recognition of these values, which is precisely what Kierkegaard asserts in his treatment of the ethical and the religious. In addition, transgression often enough takes the form of a flight into another sign system, to alternate forms of subjectivity set up in different regimes of signs, different narratives. In asserting that one could experience the present moment (indeed that one often does) without dropping it into the human time of a narrative location, one narrativizes precisely the moment that one tries to exempt from narrative. In asserting that life has no telos, one gives life a telos: letting go of project, which is project enough for anyone. But if a philosopher merely concludes effortlessly from all this that every moment of life is ethically significant, or that our experience of trees is always already an experience of symbols, he is blind or disingenuous, because the argument can and must also run the opposite way.

You would not and could not (in any case, no one does) hold up every action to ethical evaluation, unless you were continually watching the ethical content break down. The disciplines which subject us to signs must find the material (us) recalcitrant, else they would not have to break bodies to make us free. Judging every action of every one (if it were not simple lunacy) could only respond to the imposition of ethical content on material radically in excess of ethics. As I have argued elsewhere: the transgression is no transgression without a socially-driven taboo, but the taboo is impossible without the consciousness of transgression. Ethics depends on its violations to gain its content, as the police depend on criminals for employment. One would not be "humanizing" time with all the machinery of literature, trying to stop the elephant with a pop gun, unless one were aware that time was inhuman, that time wastes, kills; that time shatters narratives as well as demands them, enables you to let them go as well as to make them. One would not obsessively locate the present moment as emerging from some past and proceeding toward some future without an awareness of that moment and its strange capacities, its possibility of ecstasy, and the material in it that won't be sucked into story, that will be forgotten, perhaps by a great effort.

As does MacIntyre, Ricoeur diagnoses the view that narrative imposes order on a chaos, or artificially humanizes inhuman time as a symptom of modernity.

> [W]e may be tempted to say that narrative puts consonance where there is only dissonance. In this way, narrative gives form to what is unformed. . . . This is how it consoles us in the face of death. But as soon as we no longer fool ourselves by having recourse to the consolation offered by the paradigms, we become aware of the violence

and lie. . . . From then· on, the narrative consonance imposed on temporal dissonance remains the work of what it is convenient to call a violence of interpretation. (72)

One thing I will say for Ricoeur: he certainly states his opponent's position in a very compelling way! But his response to this view shows both how close he is to MacIntyre in his treatment of the standoff, and how far he is from MacIntyre in his treatment of narrative.

> We ought to ask . . . whether the plea for a radically unformed temporal experience is not itself the product of a fascination for the unformed that is one of features of modernity. In short, when thinkers or literary critics seem to yield to a nostalgia for order or, worse, to the horror of chaos, what really moves them, in the final analysis, may be a genuine recognition of the paradoxes of time beyond the loss of meaning characteristic of one particular culture—our own. . . . We can then legitimately suspect the alleged discordance of our temporal experience as being only a literary artifice. (72, 73)

This is a rather devastating passage, but let me assay a few replies. First, if it is asserted as an attack (as it is by both Ricoeur and MacIntyre) that their enemy's positions are bound to their time and culture, that, I propose, is trivial. So are theirs. If I'm a romantic existentialist, MacIntyre and Ricoeur are bourgeois capitalist liberals, trying to turn every moment to account, constantly punching God's time clock. Of course, Ricoeur explicitly calls his position "transcultural" and MacIntyre, at least when he's attacking modernists, appears to ascribe the same status to his own position, though according to his own position, that is a status that no position can possess.

Well, they can appeal to Aristotle, who wrote a long time ago. I could lob back Heraclitus or Parmenides, both of whom would make narrative in MacIntyre and Ricoeur's sense impossible. They could point out that all peoples tell stories, and I might come back with antilinguistic traditions such as Taoism or Zen. I suggest that both our views are more or less the product of our cultural locations. Furthermore, if I have been right about the political upshot of narrativism, their views are historically located in a context in which power operates by inscribing bodies, and in which subjects are empowered by affirming themselves to be the inscriptions to which they have been subjected.

Furthermore, though recommending chaos is, right here, a literary artifice, so is recommending literary artifice; that is, it is nothing more than a literary artifice, and by its own account. Narrativism makes of literary artifice itself a literary artifice; makes of trope a trope, of narrative a narrative. We are dealing here with a metaphorics of metaphorics; the literary device of making literary devices into the always already of human action and experience. Or as Ricoeur puts it: "Intelligibility always precedes itself and justifies itself."[6] Indeed. Or rather: indeed? Metaphorics provides a rich metaphor, we might say, but using it as Ricoeur does simply erases its status as a device, which is particularly possible in this case because it is not a particular literary device, but the device of literary device in general. The account of human time as narrative is a narrative, but at this point we get sucked so far into the self-referentiality of the sign that we are trapped and empowered by the redundancy, by our own redundancy. Accept the device of device as something more than a device or a heuristic, and one will never wander out again. Life is (literally!) a metaphor, on this view. That might sound kind of sad to people who, unlike MacIntyre and Ricoeur (and me), don't spend most of their time pawing texts. By an odd coincidence, it is professional interpreters of texts who put forward the idea that life is an interpretation of texts.

But as I have indicated, Ricoeur's account attributes to narrative resources that MacIntyre's doesn't seem to provide. Ricoeur is exquisitely sensitive to the fact (also thematized explicitly by Aristotle) that narratives (for example, tragedies) display unexpected twists and turns, shocking reversals, and so forth.

> [T]he consonance characteristic of narrative which we are tempted to oppose in a nondialectical fashion to the dissonance of our temporal experience must itself be tempered. Emplotment is never the simple triumph of "order." Even the paradigm of Greek tragedy makes a place for the upsetting role of peripeteia, those contingencies and reversals of fortune that solicit horror and pity. The plots themselves coordinate distention and intention. (72–73)

So whereas MacIntyre precisely opposes narrative to disorder (and himself opposes nothing so much as disorder), Ricoeur's project, in part, is to show how a narrative understanding of human identity, experience, action, and history can respect disorder, can "coordinate" order and disorder. In other words, whereas MacIntyre's narratives are monological, Ricoeur's are dialectical: narrative is precisely the site where the order and disorder of human life enter into a relationship, or are displayed in their interdependence. This, I think, constitutes Ricoeur's way through the standoff I have been describing.

---

6. *Time and Narrative*, vol. 2, trans. Kathleen McLaughlin and David Pellauer (Chicago: University of Chicago Press, 1985), p. 28.

And this approach allows Ricoeur to treat narrative in a much more open-ended and pluralistic way than does MacIntyre. Whereas, for MacIntyre, the narrative of one's life renders one's whole life coherent in the service of the mysterious telos, for Ricoeur the narrative inscribes both the coherence and the incoherence of one's life. And we must not leave out of account the possibility that, for Ricoeur, though narrative requires telos, that telos itself could be re-articulated or even reversed in the course of the narrative. That possibility would lend narrativism very salutary capacities indeed, and make it much "truer" to the way people experience life: we rummage around among purposes, or drift for a time without purpose, and so on. (And, in fairness to MacIntyre, he suggests something along these lines in *Whose Justice? Which Rationality?*)

Furthermore, whereas MacIntyre's treatment would seek to re-articulate a purpose (culturally emergent though it would be) for all of us, Ricoeur is also concerned with the subversive possibilities of narrative, the possibilities of counternarratives that would allow the silenced to speak.

> We tell stories because in the last analysis human lives need [to be] and merit being narrated. This remark takes on its full force when we refer to the necessity to save the history of the defeated and the lost. The whole history of suffering cries out for vengeance and calls for narrative. (75)

Indeed, the history of "liberation movements," movements which, finally, have as their telos the alleviation of suffering, shows that such movements require a rearticulation of narratives, and a seizing of or claiming of narrative. We see this in such movements as Afrocentrism, which seeks to empower black folks by taking control of the narrative of African and African-American history, or Ecofeminism, which seeks to revalue the traditional narratives of womanhood into a tool of empowerment for women and an opening into the possibility of saving the earth.

These are necessary moments and movements. And yet they too are projects. Though Ricoeur's account of narrative frees it of some of the grandiose constraints imposed by MacIntyre, it might be right to say that it strips narrative down very nearly to simple project, because it maintains the basic relation to teleology, now pluralized, but not itself problematized. Though Ricoeur opens narrative to a variety of purposes, he holds on to Aristotelian means/ends rationality in a very direct way. We evade subjection by the sign only in a perfect identification with another sign, which now becomes our always already. And with the help of Bataille, I now want to go on to throw even this opened version of narrativism into question.

II

In many ways, Bataille stands exquisitely opposed to MacIntyre and Ricoeur. Bataille found nothing as hateful as project, unless it was the ersatz coherence that project gives to a human life. I now want to consider in detail some passages from Bataille's *Inner Experience*.

> "Action" is utterly dependent upon project. And what is serious, is that discursive thought is itself engaged in the mode of existence of project. Discursive thought is evinced by an individual engaged in action: it takes place within him beginning with his projects, on the level of reflection upon projects. Project is not only the mode of existence implied by action, necessary to action—it is a way of being in paradoxical time: it is putting off existence to a later point.[7]

Bataille puts "action" in scare quotes and here's why: he is referring to action as it is conceived in the Western philosophical tradition. Paradigmatically, he is referring to action as it is explained (as MacIntyre and Ricoeur explain it) by Aristotelian practical rationality: one who wants x must do a; I want x; I will do a. This is an overweeningly teleological conception of human action, and it is worth noting at the outset that the matter of why we do what we do is as often hidden from ourselves and from one another as it is transparent.

But of course one can act in the present moment, one can move around, stuff food into one's face, and so forth, without running through any practical syllogisms. Aristotelian phronesis makes human movement a very intellectual thing, as if all human action was tied to rationality. As often as not, however, the practical syllogism is engaged only when an explanation of some action is demanded; the practical syllogism is a mode of giving a rationally defensible account of oneself, and thus is tied up with the various technologies of productivity and surveillance that make such accounts comprehensible and important. To give an account, voluntarily, is to empower oneself in a reconciliation to or identification with the sign.

On Aristotle's view, one cannot move around without muttering to oneself continually, and muttering in the sort of way that, if made public, would count as an account of oneself. Or at any rate, that is one reading of the "practical syllogism." It is MacIntyre's reading, for example, and I must say that I do think it is the best way to read the *Nicomachean Ethics*: that action proceeds by deliberation which in turn consists of an explicit course of practical reasoning. MacIntyre:

---

7. *Inner Experience*, trans. Leslie Anne Boldt (Albany: State University of New York Press, 1988 [1954]), p. 46.

On Aristotle's view the individual will have to reason from some initial conception of what is good for him, being the type of person he is, generally circumstanced as he is, to the best supported view which he can discover of what is good as such for human beings as such; and then he will have to reason from that account of what is good and best as such to a conclusion about what is best for him to achieve here and now in his particular situation.[8]

The ridiculousness of this account is sealed a few pages later when MacIntyre describes a hockey player skating down the ice with a puck in the final seconds of a game, seeing a teammate open for a shot and deliberating about whether to pass. More or less, the player will start out by asking who he is, to which he will no doubt answer, "a hockey player." Then he's going to ask what is good as such and then I guess what is good for anyone similarly circumstanced and so on until sometime early the next day he makes the pass. In fact, this is as good example as any for showing that the practical syllogism only describes the process that leads to a very small proportion of human actions, and that that is a good thing. You know what happens? The hockey player sees everything at once and then makes the pass; there's no discursive process here at all because the game's too fast. And if a sportscaster is stupid enough to ask, what were you thinking as you made the winning assist? the answer is liable to be, I wasn't thinking anything; it just happened; God blessed me. (I watch a lot of sports on television.) And yet this is (obviously) a deliberate human action. But it is an instantaneous action and is liable to be experienced as instantaneous, and this is most the case in the circumstance in which the pass was absolutely perfect or beautiful: there, the temporal smear has collapsed utterly into perfect presence.

In a discursive account of action, one's body becomes responsible to oneself as something by which or for which an account must be rendered. It is no wonder that discourse becomes central: people can and for the most part do operate without it, but people can only give an account of themselves to themselves and to others in it. Here, we simply replace the event with the account of the event. Ricoeur writes:

> The patient who talks to a psychoanalyst presents bits and pieces of lived stories, of dreams, of "primitive scenes," conflictual episodes. We may rightfully say of such analytic sessions that their goal and effect is for the analysand to draw from these bits and pieces a narrative that will be both more supportable and more

---

8. *Whose Justice? Which Rationality?* (Notre Dame: Notre Dame University Press, 1988), p. 125.

> intelligible. Roy Schafer has even taught us to consider Freud's metapsychological theories as a system of rules for retelling our life stories and raising them to the rank of case histories. The narrative interpretation implies that a life story proceeds from untold and repressed stories in the direction of actual stories the subject can take up and hold as constitutive of his personal identity. It is the quest for this personal identity that assures the continuity between the potential or inchoate story and the actual story we assume responsibility for. (74)

If Ricoeur were to hold that this account were "transcultural," his position would be laughable. His particular appropriation of Aristotle is in keeping with the institutionally demanded notion of narrative project characteristic of late modernity. That one makes of oneself a case history, and thus satisfies the demands of the psychological institutions, that one comes to experience oneself as a case history are "facts" that, as Foucault has taught us, are historically contingent and that respond to material conditions that the narrative renders invisible or is used precisely to conceal. The question has got to be: who's taking notes; where are the files, and so forth, until you are yourself taking notes and the files are in your head. Then you have become the embodiment of the disciplines of surveillance; you have become an "integrated subject," a single coherent subject conceived as a case study, as a history, as a narrative. You have reconciled yourself to your subjection, and thus become "autonomous."

This is the self conceived as a project for itself, the self conceived as a technology in the image of the technologies to which it subjected in the disciplinary archipelago. The incoherence of selves, their unnarratability is, finally, a barrier to their productivity in a service economy. The self that makes of itself a project, a case history, that files itself away in itself, is then suited to make of everything and everyone else a text and a project. This self is a narrator empowering itself by its naturalization of and participation in the narrative subjection of itself and others. That you hold every moment of your life in bondage to the chattering moralist, that you seek therapy precisely so that you may do so, and so forth, externalizes the self as social, but does so in a very particular way, or into a very particular social situation: a situation that demands an account and then inserts it into your medical record or personnel file.

Bataille connects project with discursive thought in a way, I suppose, that MacIntyre could support: there are no "projects" without an imaginary construction of the future; there is no imaginary construction of the future without discourse. But Bataille feels himself to be tortured by discursive thought, or at least by an inability to take a vacation from it and hence from his life-project. This shows us very clearly why language is central to the thought of this century. As MacIntyre notes, modernity (not to speak of postmodernity) is characterized by a breakdown of single traditions, single projects, single visions of human purpose, and so forth. The obsession with language is in part an attempt to reinstate such things in a nostalgic return to coherent meaning, or rather now as a willed imposition of meaning on the human and more-than-human world. The anxiety here is an anxiety born of imperfect subjection of the self by a single sign system; the impulse is toward order, here conceived most generally as a temporal order in narrative, but in fact expressed as a yearning for the perfect liquidation of the human and its context into the sign. The desire is to institute a sign system in which we are always already located, but what is erased are the microsystems of power to which bodies must be subjected in order to experience their own reinscription as a metaphysical necessity or as the "human condition."

Internally, it is the operation of will in conjunction with discourse, or the association of will with discourse, that makes of narrative a torture. Will in the West is the "faculty" of normalization which shows our freedom; we are empowered as wills precisely at the moment that we are perfectly reconciled to some sign system; will is the "faculty" on which practical rationality is grounded. The will wills ends, or locates the subject in human narrative time.

If MacIntyre is right, there is now no possibility of a simple recommitment to the values and projects of our culture; our culture displays no coherent set of values or projects. Thus the recommitment to project itself becomes a project; it could only be an achievement, an act of will that will make willing itself possible and univocal. Our first project is to make project possible to ourselves, which is to make ourselves possible as project: precisely the task to which MacIntyre and Ricoeur devote themselves. This is ironic, because of course modernity's methods of production are teleologically driven to an incredible extent; the debate rarely proceeds beyond the issue of efficiency. Our lives tend to get ordered as neatly as possible into a series of tasks. And that of course, after a while, is not much of a life. What is missing, as MacIntyre points out, is a life-project that orients all our other projects into a coherent narrative.

But the end of the life project provides us also with some interesting resources, some possibilities of liberation. For maybe in a realization of the self-destroying character of a life lived in projects but without Project, we can find a moment of quietude, a moment in which the boss or the Boss or the Will isn't yelling at us, or in which we're no longer listening. Maybe in the breakdown of the life-project we can re-emerge out of a total entrapment in discursive thinking, and hence out of various divisions of ourselves, and out of various power formations operating on us (in part) discursively.

One feature of a narrative mode of life is that it divides the self into speaker and listener, master and slave. This couldn't be clearer than in the philosophers MacIntyre admires: Plato, Aristotle, and Aquinas, for example. The speaker (will) commands the body forward on the quest; the body is more or less pliable, more or less recalcitrant and so forth. If perfect pliability is achieved, the subject is subject to nothing but its own will and is thus perfectly reconciled to and empowered by some regime of significance. It is no wonder that the traditions MacIntyre celebrates are dualistic traditions. The distinction between body and soul is primordially the distinction between slave and master, baseness and virtue, listener and lecturer. On the other hand, the seduction into ecstasy and the attraction of the present moment are precisely the seduction and attraction of a reconciliation of the self to the self, an implosion of a dualized self into a single thing. Whereas the normalizing reconciliation to a regime of significance resolves us perfectly into the master will in ourselves, the seduction into ecstasy reconciles us perfectly into the slave body, and hence "liberates" us in another direction. (To be a sexual sadist is to be reconciled with will; to be a sexual masochist is to be reconciled with enslavement; ecstasy rests with the latter.) That is necessarily a letting-go of discursive thought, or what Kierkegaard calls the universal, into particularity and into a kind of unity.

Of course, there are different kinds of unity here; what MacIntyre and Ricoeur are on about is the temporal unity of a self driven forward by a telos. But that form of unity, though it is a unity in time or through time, is also a fragmentation of the self. And then there is a unity of the self in the implosion into the present moment, a unity that is available to me at all times because I am at each moment in fact in that moment. But of course this latter unity is nothing like the unity of a single subject as that is conceived in the Western tradition: namely, as a discursive production transparent to itself or hearing itself perfectly (a unity achieved in perfect inscription by disciplinary regimes). What I might be in a collapse into immediacy may well be completely incoherent by that standard; I am precisely allowing myself to stop imposing coherence on myself at that moment.

Bataille says that a life lived in project or narrative or discursivity is lived in paradoxical time. That is a very pregnant remark, especially given that such thinkers as Ricoeur and David Carr think that narrative yields the only possibility of human existence in time, that narrative "humanizes" time or gives us a human time in which to persist and to understand our persistence. But the putting off of existence to a later time is indeed paradoxical, because existence cannot be deferred while we exist. That is, we are always precisely in the present moment, are living now, and not when our project is complete. That was in essence Augustine's problem about time: how to understand, in the present, existence emerging out of the past and moving into the future. Of course in the present moment I am informed by the past and possibly by a projection into the future; that is why "human" time is supposed to be narrative time. But the meaning of the present moment or its value are supposed to be held in suspension, held for the service of the future. That is paradoxical because I am existing now and not yet then.

But the time of project is paradoxical in another sense also: it seems to run backwards. We live into the present moment, or experience it, as something that proceeds out of our projection in the present moment of a future. The time of narrative thus does not, as is sometimes argued, make the experience of time for the first time comprehensible; in fact it makes a hash of time in a certain way, as if the present and the distant future, instead of the latter developing out of the former, were rushing headlong at each other in a continual collision.

This situation only becomes worse if we are attempting to locate a project sufficient to whole lives. Bataille says this about salvation:

> Salvation is the summit of all possible project and the height of matters relating to projects. Moreover, by virtue of the very fact that salvation is a summit, it is negation of projects of momentary interest. At the extreme limit, the desire for salvation turns into a hatred of all project (of the putting off of existence until later): of salvation itself, suspected of having a commonplace motive. If I, in anguish, exhaust remote prospects and inner depths, I see this: salvation was the sole means of dissociating eroticism (the Bacchic consummation of bodies) from the nostalgia for existing without delay. (47)

Salvation gives us the strongest version of the project of constructing a project for ourselves, and it defers existence entirely: defers it out of existence. Our existence would then be deferred precisely until it is impossible. The temporality associated with salvation is the most paradoxical of all, because it puts off existence until the moment of nonexistence. To say the obvious, that is a will to death, a will lurking at the heart of project, and increasing in intensity with every attempt to make our lives more unified under the auspices of teleology.

But for Bataille, first of all, the project of salvation makes all lesser or temporally limited projects seem beneath contempt; a life truly lived for salvation would have to cultivate some sort of indifference to worldly project. And hence it can bring us to despise project and narrative quite generally, so that finally it calls itself into question as a project. This is as it should be, for salvation is the beginning of eternity, an eternity without projects; salvation is the final end of project, so that what we fight for by project is the extinction of project itself.

Bataille speculates that the function of salvation here is to pit itself against eroticism, so that we are not tempted to provide ourselves with more "commonplace" methods for the extinction of project. Salvation gives us the masochist-erotic or the seduction to extinction without calling us into the present moment or into our bodies; it is the promise of an end of project as an end of sin.

Again, sin is conceived by Kierkegaard's Hegel as the assertion of particularity or the collapse into the present moment. I suggested earlier that the basic opposition is between sin and sign, that for Ricoeur the order of the sign is always already everywhere the order of ethical. It is no surprise, therefore, that the primordial sins are erotic. If life is a project, then it ends with the extinction of project; it is, in fact, the project of the extinguishing of projects, which shows us very clearly that project can be experienced as a torture. The notion of salvation tries to separate the extinction of project from the erotic seduction into sin as presence or lapse of sign, and hence to preserve the possibility of project.

Project calls us ever forward toward completion, toward a discharging of the telos. But if existence just is project, then this consummation must be continually deferred. Project calls precisely for the end of project; the right existential state in the service of project is continual impatience; projects are things we would like to get over with. To make of life a project is to make life the project of ending projects. But a lapse from the project is sin, and hence the erotic must not be allowed to seduce us from productivity. If life is a project, then the project must never lapse. But then it seems absurd to claim that life is a project, because it can never be completed.

But the alternative to salvation as project, or to happiness achieved over a whole human life, if life is a narrative in MacIntyre's sense, is precisely life as a series of finite projects. This view would be compatible with Ricoeur's position. Bataille finds that an even sadder vision.

> One has egotistical satisfaction only in projects; the satisfaction escapes as soon as one accomplishes; one returns quickly to the plan of the project—one falls in this way into flight, like an animal into an endless trap; on one day or another, one dies an idiot. In the anguish enclosing me, my gaiety justifies, as much as it can, human vanity, the immense desert of vanities, its dark horizon where pain and night are hiding—a dead and divine gaiety. (49)

We find ourselves again at the dilemma I framed earlier: either life is a welter of projects, in which case we are simply trying to find some way today to fend off the present and to fend off death, or else life is single project, in which case we live backwards from eternity into the present, seeking extinction, seeking never to have been born.

Bataille confronts project with sacrifice, a central notion in all his writings. Project means for Bataille the efficient application of energy toward a specified end, but Bataille argues elaborately (most notably in *The Accursed Share*) that our energy is, considered on the whole, wildly excessive to our ends. That is not to say that we can always achieve our ends because we always have the energy to do so; for one thing, there may be local energy deficits, and for another, not all energy can be deployed in any way. But by and large, and even by definition, energy is excessive to project, because a new project always seems to loom, or the project is indefinitely deferred and hence we must occupy our time meanwhile. So the moments of recollection into presence that Bataille evokes are moments of energy in excess to strict need, which, when expended, brings us to "the extreme limits of the possible." An example is eroticism, on which humans lavish incredible energy in excess to its procreative function.

When existence is deferred, one must find some way of expending the energy one now has: in sex, communication, sacrifice, mystical ecstasy, and so forth. Otherwise, for one thing, this energy would swamp projects entirely. The basic question for Bataille is not how our wealth is to be applied in the service of our goals, but rather how is it to be liquidated as we proceed toward our goal, and for that matter once we get there. The liquidation or consumption of the energy that is apparently held in reserve for project is always an emptying of project into the present moment; the liquidation of wealth is the annihilation of its future applications.

> The realm of morality is the realm of project. The opposite of project is sacrifice. Sacrifice falls into the forms of project, but only in appearance (or to the extent of its decadence). A rite is the divining of a hidden necessity (remaining forever obscure). And whereas, in project, the result alone counts, in sacrifice, it is in the act itself that value is concentrated. Nothing in sacrifice is put off until later—it has the power to contest everything at the instant it takes place, to summon everything, to render everything present. The crucial instant is that of death, yet as soon as the action begins, everything is challenged, everything is present. (137)

Recall Kierkegaard's treatment of Abraham's sacrifice of Isaac. God calls Abraham out of his ethical story of himself and into an immediate senseless expenditure. (Bataille: "What is substantially rejected in evil is a concern with the time to come" [*On Nietzsche*, p. 28].) He does not promise Abraham this or that if the sacrifice is performed; he simply demands the death. This liquidation of resources to no goal is at once a monstrous transgression and a call to complete presence, to the realm of the religious. The sacrifice must take the form of transgression because "the realm of morality is the realm of project."

Hence MacIntyre and Ricoeur are certainly right to connect their ethics to what they call narrative. Ethics may take the form of rules to which we have to live up (Kant), or of goals which we must pursue (Mill), or of virtues which we must cultivate (Aristotle). In all cases ethics purports to strand us in the paradoxical time of project. Existence, however, cannot be deferred; we exist right now, and present energy must be expended. The function of transgression is hence the call into the present, and every transgression is a transgression precisely in virtue of this call: it brings us to orgasm or death or mystical ecstasy, to the wanton waste of "resources." Thus sacrifice takes the form of transgression and places us in a time in which existence is not deferred. Call that time "inhuman" if you want to, or call it impossible, but every culture that practices sacrifice has a way of gaining access to it.

In the *Bhagavad-gita*, the god Krishna tells the war leader Arjuna to fight a battle not as an instrument for achieving certain ends, but as a sacrifice. That is the great mystery that the *Gita* presents the West: how to fight, but not for a telos. What Krishna says is: act now, expend energy, destroy lives, and by letting go of ends and by consecration and by transgression enter the holy present. The *Gita*, like *Fear and Trembling*, is a narrative of the letting-go of narrative. Arjuna's compunctions about fighting are ethical compunctions; Krishna's cure for these compunctions is sacrificial ecstasy and the breaking apart of rationality.

It is worth saying that, insofar as our energy cannot be stockpiled for later use, insofar as our experience cannot be stored as a commodity, insofar as presence has capacities that are not exhausted in their directedness toward the future, we are all always already located in sacrificial time. We are to that extent, like Job or Arjuna, slaves of God, or inhuman: ravished, unnarrated, ecstatic. And to that extent we are also already moments of resistance to regimes of inscription; we evade or exceed the disciplines of narrative textuality insofar as we actually exist and act in the present moment. For this reason, among others that I will survey, none of us are perfect embodiments of the narrative machine and its technologies of technology, its instruments of instrumentality. To live perfectly or effortlessly in "human" time would be to cease to exist in the present, actually to defer existence to some later time. No one of us, while he lives, is that perfectly directed toward death or is that dead. Krishna urges Arjuna to understand what is already the case, that he is already in action, and that this action is not "directed," or not perfectly expunged in its own end. Thus the project of letting go of project—the project of coming to live in sacrificial time—is a project of coming to be within what is already the case.

This is something we can want. "I wanted experience to lead where it would, not to lead it to some end point given in advance. And I say at once that it leads to no harbor (but to a place of bewilderment, of nonsense)" (3). For Bataille, as for Kierkegaard and Krishna and the Taoist masters, wandering in this way is the sacred dimension of experience, for it is our opening to our own aliveness and to the world in which are alive.

It is obvious that one thing that is at issue is a clash of religious visions: a mystical or ecstatic tradition and one that is more rationalistic and social. These traditions flow together in many places, starting in the Judeo-Christian-Moslem world with the Hebrew Bible. And they flow together notably in Pascal's *Pensées*. But one of Pacal's pressing concerns, even as he seeks a variety of proofs of God and for a Christian ethical life, is the absurdity or futility of the rational order of project. And Pascal, like Bataille, seeks to pound home the presence of the present and the impossibility of a deferral of existence:

> We never keep to the present. We recall the past; we anticipate the future as if we found it too slow in coming and were trying to hurry it up, or we recall the past as if to stay its too rapid flight. We are so unwise that we wander about in times that do not belong to us, and do not think of the only one that does; so vain that we dream of times that are not and blindly flee the only one that is. The fact is that the present usually hurts. We thrust it out of sight because it distresses us, and if we find it enjoyable, we are sorry to see it slip away. We try to give it the support of the future, and think how we are going to arrange things over which we have no control for a time we can never be sure of reaching. . . . The present is never our end. The past and present are our means, the future alone our end. Thus we never actually live, but hope to live, and since we are always planning how to be happy, it is inevitable that we should never be so.[9]

In this as in so much else, Pascal is astonishing in his modernity and in his psychological acuity. The constant deferral of presence is a flight from the present's poignancy ("the fact is that the present usually hurts"). On the most sympathetic reading of Aristotle, this criticism does not strictly apply, because the end could plausibly be held to be the present, at least in some cases (though that too lands us in various puzzles); that is, the end is happiness conceived as action

---

9. Blaise Pascal, *Pensées*, trans. A. J. Krailsheimer (London: Penguin, 1995), p. 13.

expressing virtue. Nevertheless, the picture of all human activity remains an administration of means that places time in deferral if we presume that we are not right now already perfectly happy. But the situation is even worse for, say, the pragmatists (whom I will discuss in a bit) or for contemporary analytic action theorists. If we read various configurations of practical rationality as attempts to evade the present we would have to read them also as delusions: the present can never be evaded.

For Pascal, we are trapped in an attempt to achieve rest by activity and activity by rest; he calls to his aid the story of Pyrrhus (39–40), who said that his purpose in trying to conquer the world was to rest content. As Pascal realizes, such a person will never rest content; there is no happiness if life is nothing but a quest for happiness, for the rhythm of the quest becomes perfectly ingrained, becomes a way of life.

> [People] have a secret instinct driving them to seek external diversion and occupation, and this is the result of their constant sense of wretchedness. They have another secret instinct, left over from the greatness of our original nature, telling them that the only true happiness lies in rest and not in excitement. These two contrary instincts give rise to a confused plan buried out of sight in the depths of their soul, which leads them to seek rest by way of activity and always to imagine that the satisfaction they miss will come to them once they overcome certain obvious difficulties and can open the door to welcome rest. (40)

And if the common vision of practical rationality (in Aristotle, as well) is correct, there is no point in resting content anyway; that could only mean the complete cessation of action. But Pascal's point is that even if this *is* "the human condition" (and from my point of view the most distressing claim in Pascal is precisely that it *is* the human condition; he calls it concupiscence, misery, wretchedness, fallenness), it can be relieved only in "annihilation," in becoming nothing before God, or in realizing that one is nothing before God: "Jesus wants his witness to be nothing" (3). What the theorist of practical rationality holds to be the human condition is precisely what Pascal conceives as original sin. But we cannot be fallen in this sense, cannot be perfectly fallen, because the presence of the present is also all too obvious. If the imaginary deferral of presence is typical of human beings, so is a complete immersion in the present moment. And the moment of the sacrifice or the ritual transgression is the moment in which *that* fact becomes present, in which the teleological order is compromised in a self-annihilation, in which the present comes to us like a blow and makes us see what is always already the case. This is also the moment described by Bataille: the moment of annihilation, the annihilation of language and history that is *intended* in the sacrifice.

Now as I have indicated, even the return to immediacy, or the letting-go of ends, could itself be represented as a project. It is precisely Bataille's project. Yet by the same token the continual deferral of existence in project could be taken to show that there are, finally, no projects, that every project is a delusion that lands us in paradoxical time. That every project seeks its own destruction as project, that is, its own fulfillment, tends to suck project back into the realm of the wanton waste of resources. So again we are faced with the standoff: whether to make a project of the letting-go of projects or to make sacrifices of projects, silence out of the chatter.

> And this difficulty is expressed in this way: the word *silence* is still a sound, to speak is in itself to imagine knowing; and to no longer know, it would be necessary to no longer speak. . . . [T]he words which serve only to flee, when I have ceased to flee, bring me back to flight. (13)
> And ecstasy is the way out! Harmony! Perhaps, but heart-rending. The way out? It suffices that I look for it: I fall back again, inert, pitiful: the way out from project, from the will for a way out! For project is the prison from which I wish to escape (project, discursive experience): I formed the project to escape from project! And I know that it suffices to break discourse in me; from that moment on, ecstasy is there, from which only discourse distances me—the ecstasy which discursive thought betrays by proposing it as a way out, and betrays by proposing it as absence of a way out. (59)

There is, obviously, an inherent danger in making a project of the end of project (but that is precisely project's own paradox), or in bringing silence to language. The practical problem is that one cannot silence oneself by telling oneself to become silent; one cannot be in ecstasy as one tries to achieve ecstasy, for in ecstasy we cease to seek ecstasy.

Insofar as Bataille addresses this problem, he seems to say that to seek ecstasy may finally leave me in ecstasy; that going out and hiring a street-walker (in his example), may indeed end in orgasm; that even if orgasm is your project, you leave that project behind precisely at orgasm. But later on, I will survey a different approach to the problem; I want to show how the self-understanding provided by narrative or goal is always radically inadequate to the everyday life in which we are all the time embedded, so that in some sense all projects are inadequate, and a life lived for project is delusory.

If my life were indeed a project, and hence narratable, and hence intelligible, I (or whomever is narrating) would need, first of all, to elide or expunge

or incorporate as barrier in the course of the narration those portions of my
life which are incompatible with my project, or unrelated to it. My life would
get measured by its "productivity" as that is conceived under the conditions of
the project. If my project, for example, were to become a happy man, then one
thing that would need elision is precisely the depths of my indifference, of the
unrecoverable distance that comes between myself and the people I love, myself
and my activities, myself and the applications of my talents, myself and my
virtues, myself and the sky. For this indifference, though I sometimes experience it as a great difficulty, and then again as a great solace, neither contributes
to my happiness nor constitutes a barrier to it. It simply serves itself, as if it were
a project, a project that I am continually pursuing though without intending
to, nor even, perhaps until this moment, realizing that I had pursued.

But the material of my indifference is continually available to me, because
one can care only so much about only so many things. Narrative devotes itself
to showing us what is significant, or what is important, or what is worth
remembering. But indifference devotes itself to achieving this moment within
the bounds of the possible. While I am walking around the house, I am thinking how happy it would make me to be a happy man, or how much I want a
MacArthur genius grant, or whether the sin I just now committed presents
itself as a barrier to my salvation. But I am also walking around the house. The
walls and furniture around which I move are things to which I am right now
indifferent, things omitted from the narrative as failing to signify; they don't
lend me any meaning. And yet my life is actually lived among these objects; as
I walk around, the directions I take are articulated by these objects. As I lose
myself in the narrative reverie, bringing everything I can find obsessively to the
trial of significance, my life consists of trying not to hit my shins. That is, my
existence cannot be fully deferred; I cannot exist fully in the narratable realm
of project and its paradoxical human time. Of course, if my sense of the narrative becomes too extreme, I will hit my shins, which would interrupt my narrative, so my continuing to prattle on requires some sort of minimal respect to
be paid to what is insignificant to me now.

That makes it look as though my life is lived for significance, and that the
present moment with its massed indifferences exists only as something that
could mess up the meaningful bits if I don't manage it successfully. This much
is trivial, if MacIntyre and Ricoeur are on anything like the right track: whatever life is lived *for* is its significance. But what this should show, in addition, is
that life is lived *in* insignificance, and that if we want to live significantly, we no
longer want to live. We step outside of narrative in ecstasy, craft, and so forth.
But we step outside of narrative with every step we take in every aspect of it

which is autonomic or to which we are indifferent. I imagine the Great Man bashing his shin in a reverie, and I imagine him saying: I should not have to put up with this. But that is just to say: I should no longer be a living person; I should by now be vaporized utterly into significance. The point is not to let go of project, but to see that none of us lives by and large in and for projects, except as a self-delusion and avoidance of life. We could sweep our lack of significance into a narrative, or we could sweep narratives into a lack of significance. The latter would be, I claim, a recommitment to life.

Narrative comes apart at the extremes; that is Bataille's point: it comes apart in ecstasy, in writhing pain, at death. But it has already also come apart everywhere, all the time, wherever people are breathing, or walking around, or watching TV, and not getting anywhere narratively speaking. What narrative is inadequate to is not just the shattering moment, but the moment of indifference. If such moments and functions are necessary to narrative, it must be pointed out that, on the contrary, they are necessary to narrative. You cannot narrate if you cannot breathe, so shut up for a moment and take a deep breath. Pull yourself away from significance for a moment and let yourself feel the sweet, deep, all-enveloping insignificance all around you. And take comfort in your own insignificance; take comfort in the triviality of your culture; take comfort in the triviality of your life-project and your failure in realizing it.

In MacIntyre's or Ricoeur's account, narrative has a sort of calm, magisterial sweep; indeed, they are calm, magisterial writers. But I wonder whether they, like me, have ever felt the need for meaning as a pressure, as an anxiety, and furthermore as the project of having some project, and hence as a project that can never be discharged. I live like this: busy trying to finish whatever's in front of me as quickly as possible. Then finished. Then feeling empty, subject to attack from my own head. Then inventing or accepting a new project. And so on. I work by projects toward the extinction of project, then can't live there and go on to a new one.

Where I find relief from this is in caring for my children; I actually am not trying to make them into particular sorts of people; I am not even usually trying to make myself into a particular sort of father to them. I'm trying to let them be and keep them safe, and we're all trying to have fun together. That's my entrance into ceremonial time. I have another, as well: playing music. I'm not trying to make myself into a master of the accordion or the harmonica; I'm just trying to find pleasure and some surcease from the voice in my head by playing. OK: that's still trying to do something. But the point is that the purpose is achieved precisely at the moment that it fades from awareness; those moments are the extinction of project sought by project. I guess what I'm writing this book to wish is that I could live there more, that I could play more. When I take up more and more of my past life into a narrative, I find there a distance. This effort reflects a need to put things in order, and then I lose a succession of present moments; that is, I lose precisely what I am also trying to hold into the narrative. What I am writing to recommend to myself is deeper and longer forms of immersion. The distance I purport to achieve in the narrative—when I think of myself as a character, think myself outside myself—is a distance from myself. I can take up more and more of my purported future, guide myself more and more ruthlessly, orient myself into the project more and more thoroughly, but then I lose a succession of present moments, and more and more of what I am all the while trying to render comprehensible escapes me. Would this project of project not then collapse inward on itself through a loss of its own material? Would it not drift further and further into abstraction? Would it not then become impossible to make my life comprehensible through narrative, though I make a comprehensible fantasy?

But above all I wonder, as Ricoeur converts time into "human time," and as MacIntyre converts life into project, whether these men have felt the fear and pain that motivates this scramble, and whether they have ever experienced their need as an anxiety that infects every aspect of life. For while the disciplinary matrix inscribes us, it also makes us anxious: anxious to please it, anxious to allow ourselves to be inscribed, anxious that we have not been thoroughly enough inscribed, anxious that our inscriptions have not been recently-enough updated, anxious that some present moment is not being turned to account, anxious that we are failing in our rationality, anxious that we are not perfect instruments, anxious that we are not the perfect masters of instruments, anxious at our indifference, anxious at our ecstasy, anxious of being found out, anxious of finding ourselves out, anxious of incoherence, anxious about the future of projects, anxious about living in the present, anxious about the sacred. In human time, every moment of existence is a moment of self-betrayal, a moment in which existence has not effectively been deferred.

And likewise, I wonder whether, as they drift to sleep, for example, Ricoeur and MacIntyre have ever felt the relief of allowing "human" time to lapse into presence, of allowing the telos to slip into unawareness. For such moments are not only necessary as rest and recreation, though they are necessary for that, they are necessary even to the possibility of a narrative of life; there have got to be actually experienced moments if there is to be a narrative construction. One needs a vacation precisely from—only from—project; the intensification of human time in instrumental rationality creates a particular need to lapse into ceremonial time or the time of play and gives the latter a "significance," seeks to bring the interstice in human time into the human order: the vacation is the sacrifice in service to the narrative, or in what Bataille terms the decadence of sacrifice. The vacation is the narratable sacrifice, the lapse of instrumentality allowed to us by the disciplines of human productivity and swept up by them into the productive order. Aristotle: "it seems correct to amuse ourselves so that we can do something serious . . . for amusement would seem to be relaxation, and it is because we cannot toil continuously that we require relaxation. Relaxation, then, is not [the] end, since we pursue it [to prepare] for activity" (*Nicomachean Ethics*, 13.23).

All of us participate in the making of narratives, but none of us can live wholly in narrative; none of us can even live very thoroughly in narrative. The lack of narrative is a kind of madness, but too much narrative is also a kind of madness. Perfect presence in the present is not recognizable as a *human* life, but perfect continual comprehensibility of the present in relation to the future is not recognizable as a human *life*.

The deepest human needs and their satisfactions, it seems to me, take the form precisely of a letting-go, or a languorous lapse into silence. We take pleasure in eating a good meal, but not because it leads us toward salvation, or even because it leads us toward happiness considered as a property of a whole life, but because it calls us into a present enjoyment wherein the imaginative reconstruction of the temporal flow is suspended. Inverting Aristotle, it is no more true that we relax in order to work than that we work in order to relax, that is, to stop ordering our lives by projects. And to repeat, at the heart of the narrative itself is the end of the narrative; the narrative is inconceivable without its "end," as MacIntyre insists. When we're finished, then we can relax, in eternity, it may be, or in retirement.

CHAPTER THREE

HISTORY AND MULTIPLICITY

I

The themes of sacrifice, play, and presence are all central to art. Art has no history, at least in the sense in which, for example, Ricouer thinks of history: as a teleological narrative of progress, as an arraying of forces toward some end. Art is not coming from or going anywhere; it has no point in that sense. The distinction of the Western fine arts as an isolable sphere of activity, as something of which there is history and a future (or not) in distinction from other spheres of cultural production, is what might be termed a fiction. The detachment of the Western fine arts from the full-scale context of human activities, forms of sociality, and engagements with the more-than-human world—a detachment of the sort that gets constructed in some of the overarching narratives of art history—is only apparent, and it serves very specific political and economic purposes. What this means is that art evades or exceeds the forms of practical rationality that are held to organize our experiences and orientations into past, present, and future. It means that we should stop thinking about art as driving in a certain direction, which we will watch unfold as time goes on. The proper response to the question of where we are going, it seems to me, is that we are *not* going; here we are.

There are two points I want to make about art and temporality. First, a general point: I think that art provides an alternative to a teleological organization of the human experience of time. Ricoeur and many others have argued

not only that human action and human lives are organized teleologically, but
that human history is so organized, that human history is itself a great project,
or at least that it must be represented that way in historiography. We are progressing toward or reverting away from the realization of our purposes, or of
God's purpose, or of some purpose perhaps entailed internally within the character of our activities. Historiographical time is directional in relation to some
goal or plurality of goals. I call this time "historiographical" because it makes
possible and is made possible by assembling stories or narratives of time, stories
or narratives which constitute "history" in the modern sense. Collectively, we
direct ourselves out of a past and into a future, seeking culminations understood
as locations in a linear temporality, high points on the line graph, as it were.
Now there are "histories" of art, historiographical arts, narratives of progress
and reversion and culmination. But I want to challenge such histories through
a discussion of the character of the arts; the arts provide an alternative to the
teleological ordering of time. Second, I want to challenge a very particular narrative from the same point of view: the narrative of the Western fine arts, which
are the historiographical arts *par excellence*. I will suggest that this narrative—
while it is itself historically effective, that is, while it to some extent effects the
character of artistic production—is impoverished with respect to the arts in
their worldwide scope and in some sense deeply at odds with the sort of activities for which it is meant to account.

Let me say, briefly, what I think art is. Art on my view is a form of immersion and connection; art is a way of entering deeply into relationship with nonhuman materials and with human communities.[1] One function of art is to
compromise and expand individualities, to show "atomic" selves as molecular,
created as individualities by their relations or by their place in a human and
more-than-human world. Art shows the self of the artist as a place or rather a
field of forces in that world: a zone of traversal, flight, or concretization.

All of that, I know, sounds extremely vague, though I hope it also sounds
interesting. So let me try some examples: think of the engagement of a painter
with paint; think of the relationship of John Coltrane to the saxophone; think
of the relation of a master of flirtation or gossip to the people around her. Each
of these activities is relational in a variety of dimensions: there cannot be
painters without paint; painters are defined as painters in their relations to
paint. There cannot be "John Coltrane" in a world with no saxophones. There
cannot be masterpieces of flirtation without a social context in which the

---

1. For a much more elaborate (though also in some ways provisional and unsatis-
factory) statement of this view, see Crispin Sartwell, *The Art of Living* (Albany: SUNY

activity is comprehensible, amusing, stimulating, enlivening, reprehensible. Now what I think of as the distinctive feature of art in this regard is a great intensity of relation, an immersion in which the relational character of the activity becomes all-absorbing, in which the self is absorbed consciously into its relations through a process of devoted making, through a devotion to relation.[2] A spiralling series of embedded intensities of molecular location is made possible through art: with the instrument, with the hearers, with a context of cultural production, perhaps with the cosmos or the gods.

The concept of human agency that derives from technical rationality is compromised, therefore, in artistic activity. I don't know whether you have had the experience of being "lost" in some activity, of losing a sense of individuatedness in the traditional sense, of feeling yarn taking some form under your hands, of having the next riff emerge from your horn "on its own" but also from your body, of dancing so hard in the mosh pit that you forget your separateness or lose the illusion of separateness from the other dancers. I hope you have such experiences; I will share with you that I yearn for them and find them very difficult to come by. But at any rate, those are the experiences that I think of as artistic.

Such experiences compromise agency in the traditional sense as they also compromise individuality; art is something one does in collaboration and identification with things and persons. And one way art compromises agency is by giving us access to an alternative form of temporality. The temporality of narrative and of agency and of historiography is, to repeat, a temporality ordered by project, by the manipulation of circumstances for the sake of achieving some end. Aristotle: "If someone chooses or pursues one thing because of a second, he pursues and chooses the second in itself and the first coincidentally" (*Nicomachean Ethics* 7.101). This, I think, constitutes a fundamental misunderstanding not only of art and of craft, but in some sense of human action and experience in their entirety.

In the time of project, technological or historiographical time, present resources are held in reserve, stockpiled for their future applications in the service of goals. There are two basic modes of what I will now call ceremonial time. First, there is the time associated with craft, which is in some sense teleological. Craft has a practical end. But this end is achieved precisely in and by a devotion to process and materials, by an immersion that compromises the time of project in which the present is deferred. In craft it is not too much to

---

2. This account is indebted to Ben-Ami Scharfstein, *Of Birds, Beasts, and Other Artists* (New York: New York University Press, 1989).

say that the future is held in the service of the present; that the goal is something that operates precisely as a method of intrinsic information of present
activity. In craft, one pursues ends for the sake of means, rather than vice versa;
the goal is something that makes possible and intensifies the present immersion.
This sounds paradoxical in the sense developed earlier, but in fact the time of
craft is more comprehensible than the time of project because it acknowledges
the goal as a "projection," acknowledges the presence of the present, and holds
the projection of a future at the service of that presence. The other mode of
ceremonial time is what, as we have seen, Bataille terms "sacrificial" time. In
sacrificial time, resources are expended in an ecstatic collapse back into the present moment. To perform a sacrifice, or to act in a sacrificial mode, is to engage
ceremonially or artistically in the trangressive and "senseless" squandering of
resources. Hence, the sacrifice is a derangement of teleological time, if a teleological time has already been established; the sacrifice is a letting go of goals for
the sake of an immersion in the present moment in devotion. The sacrifice may
indeed be performed for certain purposes: to appease the gods or forestall their
wrath, to cure sickness in the human body or the body of the world. But it
achieves these purposes by calling us to immediate absorption and identification, by a shattering of agency that also expresses humility. The two modes of
ceremonial time are interrelated, because the ceremony encodes a sacrifice, and
the sacrifice requires items made with devotion.

Art, on my view, happens in ceremonial time rather than in the time of
project. Art happens in a devotion to things that calls its maker into the present
moment and articulates for its maker modes of relatedness. Art is, in that sense,
ceremony, and ceremony is in fact inconceivable without art; we need the ritually significant objects, which are to be made or found with devoted skill, and
we need the proper forms of social relation, which we make together by a certain attentiveness not only to the proper forms, but to the expression of those
forms in the current social situation. A ceremony that does not absorb the par-
ticipants and configure their relations is a failed ceremony; the ceremony must
create and heighten forms of sociality, must create and heighten a present in
which these forms are articulated. We must be resurrounded and hence remade.

So, first of all, I count as art anything that is made in ceremonial time. This
entails that any activity at all that yields very intense configurations of relatedness, intense immersions and identifications, is potentially an art. Making love
is an art because it is an intense molecularization of the self. The crafts are arts
because they make practically useful objects by an immersion in materials and
processes. In Zora Neale Hurston's great books and essays, such things as lying,
arguing, fighting, and preaching are described as arts when they are engaged in

with joy and devotion.[3] If you are not only fighting to win, but are fighting to fight, and if you fight with the sort of skill which derives from a devotion to the process, then you are an artist. The crafts are arts. The popular arts are arts. The arts of devotion, still vital in our cultures, are arts. And so on.

The "history" of the Western fine arts in this context is a blip. You don't have to go to Soho to see art: maybe your grandmother is a quilter; maybe there's an African-American Baptist Church in your neighborhood; maybe you watch MTV. Relax. That's the real stuff, because it's fully engaged in the culture, in making and remaking relationships, in providing opportunities to take a break from our life projects and immerse ourselves in materials and in one another, maybe to take flight from where we are to another zone of the material and the cultural and the devotional.

The issue of teleology is a particularly conflicted one with regard to the Western fine arts of the last three centuries. On the one hand, it is only in teleological time that these arts have been firmly distinguished from the crafts and the popular arts: given their own history, and regarded as a separable sphere of human activity. It is a familiar point that "art history" in this sense only becomes possible with the German idealists, and above all with Hegel. The idealist cosmology is teleological: Hegel's central assertion is that the universe is driving somewhere, is coming to fruition in self-awareness. And Hegel locates art as a moment in this unfolding or intensifying or perfection of the self-consciousness of the universe, as the location in which the sensuous is spiritualized, in which base matter comes to participate in the becoming-conscious of the world. Thus, for Hegel, art is something that transcends the material and which will be transcended in its turn as itself material. So Hegel organizes arts into periods by the approximation of these periods to the transcendent project, and he describes the development of the arts, first, as inevitable, and second, as constituting an autonomous realm of human activity with an autonomous function. Finally, he discusses the end of art in both senses of the word: the culmination of its purpose and its surcease. Art then becomes historical in the strong sense: its actions are organized like the actions of an individual person allegedly are: as a project. Art becomes an agent, something that acts by moving toward a goal.

So the necessary condition of art history as it has been practiced in the West until recently is the claim that art unfolds as a development toward a goal. For a century and a half, this goal was held to be the purification of the arts

---

3. See, e.g., *Mules and Men* (New York: HarperCollins, 1990 [1935]), and the essays collected in *The Sanctified Church* (Berkeley: Turtle Island, 1981).

from extra-artistic content. That would show the character of art in a crystalline purity; one could indeed think of this as art becoming conscious of itself. And this movement is, in its lineaments, Hegelian, as Arthur Danto has shown:[4] it is an apparent purging of the material for the sake of transcendence. So we had, in the plastic arts, a movement toward abstraction and formalism. We had in literature the "intentional fallacy" and various dissolvings of reference. We had in music, first, a rejection of the "program" or representational content, and then a rejection of the suspicious pleasures aroused by tonality. Around these developments, the "artworld" of the West has reconfigured itself from an element in craft guilds to an avant-garde, from a set of crafters to a set of geniuses, from a set of practices devoted to producing useful or ritually significant items including adornments to a set of institutions that distinguish the arts as a specific zone in which utility is supposedly placed in suspension. On principle, the artworld excludes the untrained or "naive" or "primitive" in its own culture, while acknowledging the "pure abstract power" of the "primitive" in other cultures, from which it yanks artifacts out of their contexts of making and use. It incorporates the African mask and extrudes, say, blues or country music. This allows it just the hint of life and breath while it continues to hold itself separate from its own cultural context.

Thus, teleology has been necessary to detach the fine arts from the cultural scene. But strangely enough it is precisely in the suspension of teleology that this detachment is supposed to be comprehensible. In order to have a history, art must constitute itself as a separate realm with a separate momentum. But in order to constitute this realm *as* separate, art must detach itself from the grubby everyday realm of human purposes: from sex, money, and power. To that end, we invent "disinterested pleasure," "psychical distance," and the like. To that end we institute the distinction between art and craft. To that end we purge our work of representational content. In brief, we invent modernism.

So we could say that the ideology of modernism exists in a huge unreconciled tension with teleology: on the one hand, art is precisely what has no purpose; on the other, art can only be constituted as a separate realm by a distinctive teleology. So we seek moments of perfect immersion in the present, moments of a perfect letting-go of project, and we seek these precisely as a project. We pursue the sensuous as a means of surpassing the sensuous, ogle nudes as a symbol of our transcendence of sexual desire, become pure by a collapse precisely into the sacrificial transgression in which resources are senselessly

---

4. For example, in *The Philosophical Disenfranchisement of Art* (New York: Columbia University Press, 1986).

expended. In the ideology of modernism, art retains its relation to ceremonial time, but this time is swept up into a teleological order. This is another example of what Bataille calls the "decadence" of sacrifice, when the sacrifice, beyond being a squandering of resources to something, becomes a squandering of resources for something, when God becomes an imperialist, and when all time, even the time of sacrifice, is the time of project.

Furthermore, modernism occurred in a similar tension with forms of relation. As I have said, subjectivities are multiplied and compromised in art. Art draws us to the realization of the self as relational; it establishes relations to things, to persons, to the gods. Modernism uses precisely these means to intensify atomic subjectivity; the "genius" is above all the intensely self-involved subject, the great individual, the person no one else understands. And through it all, his genius is established by his total immersion in materials and his profound effects on others. Thus, modernism draws sacrifice into project, and draws relationality into self-enclosed subjectivity. The arts are in that way the cusp or node of modernity as a whole; the sacrificial relationality of the arts must be colonized by project and agency if project and agency are to become a dominant form of life.

This leads us into a very familiar critique of modernism. First, its "purity" serves class interests; it constitutes the sacrificial mode of the wealthy and an index of their spirituality. It puts the deepest immersions in materiality and sociality to the service of transcendence and individuality. It displays for perfectly determinate purposes the suspension of purpose. Technological capitalism is the most teleologically-oriented mode of production known to man: everything is measured by output, efficiency, "competitiveness." The accusation against capitalism has always been that it is dirty, that it strands us in a world in which human project sweeps everything before it. Capitalism must, therefore, appropriate ceremony and its temporality, must turn them to account, just as democracy must produce autonomous agency. For none of us, while we live, can live very thoroughly in project. Existence cannot be deferred; the present moment is always coming to us with its demands; we hunger in the present moment, or need to take a leak, or need to negotiate the traffic jam. The present moment and its mundane demands and sacrificial capacities would be expunged in a perfectly projected time. That is why projected time is paradoxical; it seeks its consummation in a moment that has not arrived, seeks erasure of the present moment as a mere means. But presence resists erasure; the body can be immolated, but it cannot now be immolated into the future.

The present moment is always present; it always presents us with *its* demands, always constitutes a barrier to project, always threatens project with extinction or ecstasy or routine. It is there, or rather here. And so in an economy and an ethics and a polity devoted to project, the sacrifice must be swept into project's law; the nonteleological must be swept lock, stock, and barrel into the teleological order. A spirituality of project is required, a sacrifice to and for project is demanded. When someone drops forty million dollars on a van Gogh, he is engaged in an attempt to liquidate resources into sacrificial time, and hence to display his overcoming of the grubby commercial world. But on the other hand he sweeps this sacrifice into an institutional/teleological context that itself constitutes and demarcates a project, constitutes and demarcates art as a project, constitutes and demarcates sacrifice as a project. The institution constitutes art; there is no Western fine art without the artworld, as Danto has taught us. This is because the institution makes possible the teleological suspension of teleology. Art can then be "pure" and be a center of power; can both serve as a badge of the transcendence of commerce and as a commercial center. The art institutions are large bureaucracies which function along the power axes that such bureaucracies do. They try to construct or inscribe the persons they embed. They legitimate or delegitimate whole fields of cultural production as arts, control their funding, surveil their producers, elicit productions that they can recognize and sweep into their projected time and their conception of agency. They provide badges of class membership or of prestige in the name of purity and transcendence.

I guess this is what I see as hopeful in postmodernism. Here, at a minimum, we get a multiplication of teleologies. What Danto calls "posthistorical art" is art that cannot be held within a single history, art that has become sick of its own story and seeks lines of flight. Postmodern art is made for political purposes, or psychological purposes, or for the sake of racial or gender or sexual identifications, or to destroy those identifications or to set them spinning. Postmodern art gives us, in addition, a vertiginous profusion of rapprochements between the art world and the wider culture. It exploits modes of involvement with works that are incompatible with the distanced regard of high modernism.

I will mention one specific artist. Rirkrit Tirivanija makes pieces out of food and the means of preparing it and the people who make it and eat it. In one exhibition, he turned a gallery inside-out, putting all the stuff from the offices in the display area and making and serving food in the rear. In another piece, he took a bike trip in Spain with a portable kitchen, stopping along the way to prepare and serve food. He thinks of the people that occupy his "environments" as part of the piece (the materials lists include "lots of people"). If he sells a piece consisting, for example, of a bunch of ingredients and pots and pans for making Thai food, he insists that the person who buys it has to use it.

Here are a some things that Tiravanija says about his own work:

> I made *Pad Thai* and put it into a vitrine. After the end of the show
> it was taken out of the case and stored away. Everything was
> kept. . . . I never thought about having to sell my work, or that
> someone would buy it. As time passed, I said, look, if somebody
> wants this thing, the only way to have any relationship to it is to
> redo it, which means to re-make the meal and put it back into the
> vitrine. . . . Basically I started to make things so that people would
> have to use them, which means if you want to buy something you
> have to use it. It doesn't have to be all the time. It's not meant to be
> put out with other sculpture or like another relic and looked at, but
> you have to use it. I found that was the best solution to my contra-
> diction in terms of making things and not making things. Or try-
> ing to make less things, but more useful things or more useful rela-
> tionships. [F]or me it's the fingerprints, and it's the drip, and it's the
> thing falling apart that makes it much more valuable than it being
> kept and preserved—it has to have a life, or has to have a history for
> it to become something. It's because all of these people have
> touched it and used it that it becomes animated. Essentially all the
> marks are the recording of its life . . . which is something museums
> try to fight. . . . You have to think about how to undermine the sit-
> uation before it undermines you.[5]

Postmodernism at its best, as in Tiravanija's work, is a decentering of art,
a collective attack on the narrative of art history. We are floundering, gloriously
it seems to me in some ways, through an era in which meanings are breaking
down. Directions are multiplied and hence directionality itself is compromised;
if everyone is moving in a different direction, then there is not any direction in
which we are all moving. That is also the nature of craft (though I have some
reservations here); it had to be extruded from art history because of its profusion of micro-teleologies. Art is flying into creative subcultures, is finding or
making microzones of becoming. And whereas dominant languages and narratives are dead, are museum pieces, are already over by the time they are dominant, these microzones of resistance and cultural formation are alive.

The English of the *Chicago Manual of Style* and the OED are dead, but the
English of slangs, whether the slangs of African America, of rural southern
America, of gay America, or of morally despised groups such as prostitutes or
drug addicts or practitioners of sado-masochism or bikers or the people who
make "Ren and Stimpy" are alive. Such vernaculars invite or seduce us into
transgression and hence sacrifice and hence immersion and hence art, as they

---

5. "En Route," *Parkett*, no. 44, 1995, pp. 116, 117.

articulate forms of social immersion and connection for their practitioners; their livingness as cultural contexts, whatever their drawbacks, is a call away from dominant narratives, perhaps into narratives of resistance, but also into the realms of the unnarrated. And all of these vernaculars and subcultures are made possible as fields of becoming of the artworld in postmodern or posthistorical art.

On the other hand, let me also say what I find problematic about postmodernism. First of all, postmodernism is above all and self-consciously a mode of discourse. If I have been right in contrasting narrative and ceremonial time, then postmodernism multiplies narratives but does not itself throw narrative time into question (in that sense it opposes itself to craft). If everyone more or less has an agenda, which is one the most familiar criticisms of postmodernism, then it is not as though agenda itself were at stake in the artistic transaction. The point is that postmodern art continues the humanization of human beings and human productions even as it multiplies subjectivities. Postmodern art is an urban art and a discursive art—an art that has lost contact with a more-than-human world. (I admit that these are crass generalities, and that there are plenty of exceptions.) Contrast, in this regard, postmodernism with ongoing craft traditions, with ongoing spiritualities such as those found among the Lakota or among the practitioners of Vodun. These traditions, which are vital right now, are actual centers of artistic production in cultures, and postmodernism has only increased the tendency of modernism to devalue and ignore them, or to appropriate them into discursive regimes.

You have perhaps detected a touch of the jargon of Deleuze in the foregoing, and now I'm going to hit it hard. That art is being deterritorialized, slipping out of its dominant narrative, in postmodernism is a good thing. But it is also simultaneously reterritorializing neglected or despised, yet vital, cultural zones. Art in postmodernism is both compromising itself as a teleological narrative and as a dominant discourse and appropriating resistant cultures and discourses into itself. It is both short-circuiting its own destruction by incorporating into the institutions what is alive and filled with possibility and compromising the museum context, flouting the expectations of its own patrons, and so on. It is both killing what is most alive in our cultures and enlivening itself. Depending on an incredibly complex set of circumstances, Western fine art will collapse under the weight of its accumulated teleology, or it will sweep all before it into that teleology and make any resistance hopeless.

One little crux of this tension was the 1993 Whitney Biennial, which was short on painting and sculpture and long on video, short on "aesthetic" art and long on "political" art and stuff that couldn't be clearly classified as art or as nonart. It was art because, for God's sake, it was in the Whitney; it was not art because, for God's sake, it wasn't "aesthetic," didn't solicit our contemplation, and so on. It was a moment at which the question of whether art still existed was present very acutely. It still existed because there was a Whitney Biennial; it didn't still exist because the Biennial was incoherent and historically discontinuous and was itself in some sense opposed to art. Art was either in the process of collapsing and hence becoming everything else in the culture, or it was in the process of eating everything. If art absorbs the massed and conflicted teleologies that it includes at the moment, then we are in for a long, strange resistance. But if art is collapsing into and becoming in every mode of cultural production simultaneously—in advertising, in pop music, in the Rodney King video (which was played on a loop at the '93 Whitney), in craft, in private, in public, in your face, in your kitchen, and in your bedroom, in short, everywhere—then art is ceasing to exist and in the process getting more and more interesting.

I said a while ago that Western art has been deeply conflicted about teleology and temporality, that it seeks a teleological suspension of teleology or the suspension of project as a project. And for the most part, postmodern art is also conflicted about teleology and temporality, but in a different sense. Modern art deployed a single temporality to sweep up into itself and transcend routes of escape from teleology; that is, it annexed ceremonial time to projected time, annexed to a transcendent narrative the places where sacrifice happens. Postmodern art deploys local teleologies in order, among other things, to break down the transcendent narrative order. The temporalities it furnishes are parallel, as it were simultaneous, but they proceed at different rates of speed. Or better, the postmodern arts display a multiplication of parallel temporalities which emerge into the artworld out of different cultural locations. So the territorialization of the artworld by subcultures with their various agendas, various festive or suicidal or political concerns, multiplies the possible forms of temporality that can appear within the institution. This might end by melting or multiplying the institution itself by compromising hegemonic time.

So my question is this: if we multiply teleologies in order to reterritorialize Teleology from its peripheries, can we achieve thereby a lapse back into the time of ceremony? Is a multiplication of teleological temporalities a route back to the present? One criticism of events such as the '93 Biennial, again, is that they are driven by agendas, that the art is polluted by purpose, that it is ideological, that it is leftist propaganda. This is a pollution because art is still conceived (now, nostalgically) as the suspension of purpose. That, recall, *is* its purpose. If minoritarian expression, and the becoming-minority of the dominant culture, can be inscribed in a leftist ideology of the arts as politically effective in a certain direction, then art can again be swept up into the time of project. Then modernism appears, paradoxically enough at this point, as it did at its beginnings, as a liberation, as a zone of unhindered expression, and so forth. But if art can become political in many contradictory ways simultaneously, can launch itself simultaneously in many directions, then art will have again resisted narrativization and projection. And if it can do that, then it may again open us to a ceremonial time that is not in turn placed at the service of project.

And so I propose to you the arts of the ordinary, the arts of letting things be. I propose a multiplication of purposes, and I hope for a collapse of purposiveness in its hegemonic forms. I propose to you an art that is perfectly for sale, that can be turned to a thousand different tasks and purposes, an art that lets itself be had. I envision an artworld that is a site of the construction and destruction of communities, that is impossibly fragmented, that is diseased, in pain, crying out, letting go. I propose to you that we make a sacrifice of the museum, that we liquidate its eternality into multiple temporalities. I propose that we sing some blues, knit some sweaters, tattoo some skin. I propose that we worship our gods and our earth with devoted skill and with ecstasy in our bodies. I propose that we enter the future by finding a hundred ways out of history, a hundred transgressions and a hundred sacrifices.

II

In all these respects, postmodernism resembles multiculturalism, or maybe one is part of the other. Multiculturalism is a multiplication of narratives and hence of teleologies and hence of temporalities. In my own practice it has been the attempt to read and hear and maybe think my way out of the narrative of the "Western tradition," to try to find a way into Chinese, Indian, Native American, African, or African American reflection. I go out looking for stuff I like in each of these traditions, and I am able to find that stuff fairly easily, because I hate "my own" tradition, which is roughly to say that I hate myself. More accurately: I hate the account we give to ourselves of "our" tradition as I hate the account I give to myself of myself. Or let me try that yet again: I hate the fact that we are compelled to give an account of ourselves, make ourselves coherent, and bow before a canon, as I hate the fact that I am compelled to give an account of myself to myself, to make sense of myself, to pretend I cohere, or to impose coherence on myself. So I'm always rummaging around for alternatives, for ways of compromising myself. I'm looking to escape myself, or my account of myself, or my compulsion to impose an account on myself—looking for leverage on my tradition or the self-understanding of that tradition, and leverage thereby also on myself and my own self-understandings.

The possibility and the political advisability of multiculturalism is conditioned by a variety of factors, of which the most obvious is an ever-increasing
fluidity of cultural production. That means increased availability of translations,
anthropological studies, and so forth. But turning aside from commonplaces
about how the world is getting smaller, cultures have always been fluid, and
anyone's cultural location is a zone in what Deleuze would call a rhizome, a
location criss-crossed by nomadic lines of ingress and egress, by deterritorial-
izations and reterritorializations, by the blooming or dying away of little linguistic zones. Western philosophy is sometimes thought of as a coherent, directional development, an oak growing from the Greek acorn. But Greece itself
was criss-crossed by cultures; the Greek language was a mess, just like all of the
Western languages, just like all languages. Europeans and European-Americans
are the speakers of languages whose origins are unrecoverable, languages that
are African, Asian, Native American, as well as European. And each of these
locations is in turn indefinitely multiple, volatile, and always in the process of
being compromised. There has never been a moment in "our" history that was
clear in its cultural location, pure in its cultural identification.

So we have always been in a "multicultural" situation, or, more deeply, in
a situation in which the individuation of cultures is never fully possible, in
which every culture is always in the process of being invaded by barbarians, or
in the process of the barbaric invasion of someone else, always in the process of
emigration, trade, intermarriage, linguistic interchange, impositions of and resis-
tances to linguistic power. Each culture embeds and is embedded in various
subcultures, dominant cultures, satellite cultures; every culture is developing out
of and into other cultures. Each culture is always in use and in question in a
variety of other cultural locations, is always being appropriated or eliminated,
always flowering in microlanguages and subcultures or condensing into death,
always being purified and polluted. There is never a moment of cultural origi-
nation, so that we could strip ourselves of accretions and return to a pure origin or language or cultural identification.

If you're willing to buy all of that, you should also be willing to buy the
claim that "the Western tradition" is a fiction, though a fiction that gets
enforced in various ways and that has concrete effects. "The Western tradition"
is a story we tell ourselves or that gets told at us that has certain political and
economic motivations and consequences. Again, we philosophers like to trace
our problems and our discourse in more or less an unbroken line to the Greeks,
which is really a joke. There are no unbroken lines anywhere in the world, and
I'll just share with you my feeling that Plato and Aristotle are more alien to me
than anything I've found in China or among the Lakota. That's not surprising:

think seriously for a minute about what there is between us and the Greeks. "The Western tradition" is a trope of racial/intellectual purity that is always luridly false to the situation at hand. Consider, for example, Heidegger's approach to the "Western tradition" in relation to his Nazism. His notion that "Being" begins with the beginning of Greek philosophy and unfolds with the history of Western philosophy is the imagining of an ethnic cleansing.

We white American academics often pretend that our culture is the direct inheritor of Europe, as if, for example, American culture were not deeply African. But we are located not only in a Western tradition, but in an African diaspora, itself a plural and contested location. And then we act as though the Western tradition was itself not in part African in origin, or as if Europe had not been criss-crossed by Huns, Turks, Mongols, Visigoths, Moors, to the point at which there is no possibility of culturally univocal origins, univocal languages, univocal ideas, univocal systems. Questions keep arising along the following lines: is African-American culture African, or is it American? It ought to be obvious that that's not the sort of question to which we could expect an answer, and we should wonder what it means that we want to ask it. Asking that question is just a way of presupposing that there is an American culture, and that it is a white culture, a European culture. We ask: Is African-American English a dialect, a slang, a vernacular, or a language? as if questions like that had answers. But each answer that is proferred takes up a certain political location: We say that Black English is parasitic on English English, and what we mean is that these folks are dependent on us. Or we say that it's an independent dialect, and we mean that their cultural construction is not exhausted by our construction of them. Or we say, finally, that we white folks at this point also speak black English, and what we mean is that the cultural constructions are mutually dependent. White English has become and is in the process of becoming black English; black slang is where American English becomes.

My point is that, aside from finding interesting texts elsewhere, and aside from finding texts that confirm or are amazingly similar to the texts of "our" tradition, multicultural practice can show us that "our" tradition is a fictional construction, can reveal to us the content of that construction, and can challenge that content. When I go on safari for the philosophically exotic, I do it primarily to assault myself, to challenge myself, to rip apart my own little narrative of myself and my tradition. I am hunting myself: looking for myself and killing myself. I want to multiply my senses of my own locations. I want to become something and someone else, or to understand that I am not what I take myself to be. If I am going out to appropriate your thought, or to bring it back to my discourse, in which I now purport to speak for you, I am engaged in the most pathetic self-delusion. And such delusions pull intellectual production into the gravitational field of the power structure that uses the "Western tradition" as an instrument of domination. Single languages, literary traditions, and so forth are templates of possible oppressions; they are constructed out of their exclusions for the purpose of further exclusions; they attempt to purify themselves by shunting their pollution elsewhere. This purification is also a kind of suicide, the construction of something frozen in time, or with a stable retrospective content. "The Western tradition" is by definition dead—a monument, a mummy; it is made by extruding from itself every location at which it becomes. Students, you'll notice, by and large hate being subjected to the Western canon; they have an instinctive suspicion of that which, in time, tries to detemporalize itself or detach itself from the conditions of its own becoming.

Multiculturalism, then, can be a terrible political error. A lot of multicultural practice consists in going out and finding or manufacturing "similarities" until we're all just one big happy family. It turns out that all traditions sound the same universal themes. Now that just makes reading Chinese philosophy or whatever redundant. And furthermore it's simply a way of legitimating our own tradition; we use a construction of you simply to redouble our own domination. So there are three options: First, if our project is representing you, especially if you are someone who has been colonized or exploited by the "representatives" of "the West," then we are much better off shutting up and trying to make room for you to speak for yourself. Second, if our project is simply to add fuel to our own fire, or to find the "universally human," that move ought to be regarded with great suspicion. The white man has always conceived himself to be neutrally human, and to speak universally (think of Descartes, Kant, and other ectoplasmic apparitions). That's a delusion we deploy to empower ourselves over people. But third, there is the possibility of using material from other traditions to come to an awareness of our own bizarre pretensions, such as the pretension to speak on behalf of what is neutrally human. A fairly responsible use of remote cultural materials is as a therapy for ourselves.

The "Western tradition" is the only place you find mind/body or culture/nature dualisms (which are, of course, the same dualism) in clear or virulent forms. These dualisms are related also to "rationality" and hence to narrative conceived as MacIntyre and Ricoeur conceive it. There are a lot of ways to throw those things into doubt, and there are many "Western" figures who have attacked them (Emerson and Dewey spring to mind). But in African or Native American thought you find expressions that are anterior to or just outside these conceptualities. I'd suggest, for example, reading *Black Elk Speaks* or, again, Zora Neale Hurston's essays in aesthetics. Now think about this: the separation of mind from body, of will from recalcitrant material, culture from nature, is delusional. Furthermore, it articulates certain definite forms of political oppression. Our construction of the "savage" or the "primitive" is a dualism: we associate ourselves with mind and culture, them with body and nature. And if you think all that's over, you haven't been paying attention to the state of American race relations. Thus, when I say that "the Western tradition" is trope of racial purity, I don't only mean that it's a fictional purgation of "alien" influences, but that its specific character is generated in specific forms of racial construction and exclusion.

If we're going to emerge from the horror of narrative ethics (alright, I admit there are worse horrors), maybe the first step (I am going to insist that it is *only* a first step) is the multiplication of narratives and of temporalities. MacIntyre is explicit in his nostalgia for the Western tradition, the time when everything was comprehensible, swept up into a single telelogical tsunami. Well, if what I've been saying is anything like right, that's fantasy, not nostalgia. But the more serious point at which I've also been hammering is that it's a nostalgia for death, if such a thing is possible, because it seeks to isolate language from the locations at which it becomes. Now the reader may have already cottoned to the fact that I owe that insight to Deleuze and Guattari, so let's let them expand on it a bit.

> Subtract and place in variation, remove and place in variation: a single operation. Minor languages are characterized not by overload and poverty in relation to a standard or major language, but by a sobriety and variation that are like a minor treatment of the standard language, a becoming-minor of the major language. The problem is not the distinction between major and minor language; it is one of becoming. It is a question not of reterritorializing oneself on a dialect or a patois but of deterritorializing the major language. Black Americans do not oppose Black to English, they transform the American English that is their own language into Black English. Minor languages do not exist in themselves: they exist only in relation to a major language and are also investments of that language for the purpose of making it minor. . . . Conquer the major language in order to delineate in it as yet unknown minor languages. Use the minor language to *send the major language racing*. (*A Thousand Plateaus*, pp. 104–105)

On this account, the minor language appears to be "parasitic" on the major language, as the transgression appears to be parasitic on the taboo. (Notice, too, that African American English is transgressive when it is used in white institutions, in institutions dedicated to inscribing the major language on bodies.) But that would be a serious misinterpretation. In fact the dependence runs more clearly the other way; the major language depends on its deterritorialization for life, even as it seeks in that same process to reterritorialize the satellite or colonized tongue. (This I guess is the same old dialectic of master and slave, dressed for the postmodern ball.) What is static or stable is dead; the soul is the principle of life and of motion. And bodies live by the acts of reterritorialization (ingestion, for example) by which they are all the time being deterritorialized by other bodies. Likewise, a language that is not in the process of being deterritorialized is literally a dead language, like Latin, say; it more or less just sits there in a haughty detemporalized grammatical grandeur.

What this is going to mean is that the condition for the existence of a major language, or of the narrative ordering of time is, precisely as we have seen, the disintegration of that language or that narrative, here conceived as the diffusion into minorities that set it racing.

> The notion of *minority* is very complex, with musical, literary, linguistic, as well as juridical and political, references. The opposition between minority and majority is not simply quantitative. Majority implies a constant, of expression or content, serving as a standard measure by which to evaluate it. Let us suppose that the constant or standard is the average adult-white-heterosexual-European-male-speaking a standard language. It is obvious that "man" holds the majority, even if he is less numerous than mosquitoes, children, women, blacks, peasants, homosexuals, etc. Majority assumes a state of power and domination, not the other way around. It assumes the standard measure, not the other way around . . . at this point everything is reversed. For the majority, insofar as it is analytically included in the abstract standard, is never anybody, it is always Nobody . . . whereas the minority is the becoming of everybody, one's potential becoming to the extent that one deviates from the model. (*A Thousand Plateaus*, 106)

It is not only right, then, to say that what I seek in multicultural practice is to escape myself and my culture and my narrative, to assault or destroy myself; one might say, and mean the same thing, that I seek to become myself, which is also to say that I seek to become someone or something else. Deviation from the "standard" is necessary to any becoming whatsoever, not because I start as the standard but because the standard is static or atemporal. That places the standard narrative or the narrative as standard into paradoxical time, as if we had, to be temporal, already to be in the future, as if the deferral of the moment was a necessity of agency, or as if we had to survey the temporal unfolding all at once in space (that was Bergson's insight). The standard is conceived as atemporal; that is its primordial function, as in Plato's Forms: what becomes is unreal, which is finally to say that we are unreal. The narrative *can be displayed*, elucidated as a spatial structure or timeline, mapped, encompassed in historiography, encased or casketed between the covers of a book.

One way to see that time has been standardized or spatialized when it is rendered into historiography involves us in another temporal paradox: that in historiographical time the present of the historian causes the past events which the historian is narrating. This is central, for example, to Hegel's philosophy of history, to Danto's, and to Ricoeur's, and it follows almost trivially out of the project of "humanizing" the past. Danto's example is this sentence: "The author of *Rameau's Nephew* was born in 1715."[6] Obviously, one would be in no position to write a sentence like that in 1716 unless one were a seer, that is, unless one comprehended time as if it were space. One might put the matter like this: Diderot's composition of *Rameau's Nephew* somewhere down the line causes it to be the case that the author of *Rameau's Nephew* was born in 1715. And of course we all produce sentences along these lines all the time ("I met my wife in college," "That was the beginning of the end," and so on). Ricoeur draws this conclusion:

> *There is no history of the present*, in the strictly narrative sense of the term. Such a thing could only be an anticipation of what future historians might write about us. The symmetry between explanation and prediction, characteristic of the nomological sciences, is broken at the very level of historical statements. (*Time and Narrative*, vol. 1, 147)

Or putting it a bit more strongly: in historiography there is no present. Or: history divests each narrated moment of its presence. Now there are wilder ways of doing history than this suggests, but we are returned here to the result we arrived at earlier: to narrate an event is to divest it of its presence, but the succession of presents is precisely the material out of which the narrative is constructed, so that there is a momentum in the narrative toward becoming a "structure" or a "standard," an arid atemporal chart that ceases precisely to be the history *of* anything and begins to serve its own demands. There has been a general conflict in the theory of historiography for many years between proponents of "scientific" and proponents of "narrative" models. Speaking from outside the discipline I am more interested in their subterranean allegiances and mutual dependencies than in their contrast. While it is often argued that narrative history respects temporality in a way that scientific history does not

---

6. Arthur Danto, *Narration and Knowledge* (New York: Columbia University Press, 1985), p. 12.

(and while that is true to some extent), I am interested in the ways that narrative history also vitiates time by rendering it fantastically into an instrument. In historiography there is no present, because once the historian locates her own narrative position with regard to the past, her own presence is sucked away into the future as well. So history, we might say, becomes pure project—time in infinite deferral. Nothing is happening now. Because we are oriented prospectively with total ruthlessness, we live only retrospectively. What is happening today cannot be known until tomorrow, but the interpretation given tomorrow of today is indeterminate until the day after tomorrow, and so forth. If I may venture a conclusion out of this: we live on the earth and not in history. History is precisely what never happened or never happens yet, so it is hard to see how *it* can be narrated. We are going to be much better off with modest localized incomplete teleologies, but as long as the fundamental form of life is conceived to be teleological then nothing can happen, because existence is always in deferral.

One result of this destruction of the pastness of the past is that—since no moment can be known until it is over, and the knowing of that moment cannot be known until the knowing is over, and so on—the past appears infinitely malleable. What is past can be made the object of will; it can be reappropriated as a resource. Its fatality is expunged. Richard Rorty writes:

> The drama of an individual human life, or of the history of humanity as a whole, is not one in which a preexistent goal is triumphantly reached or tragically not reached. Neither a constant external reality nor an unfailing source of inspiration forms a background for such dramas. Instead, to see one's life, or the life of one's community, as a dramatic narrative is to see it as a process of Nietzschean self-overcoming. The paradigm of such a narrative is the life of the genius who can say of the past, "Thus I willed it," because she has found a way to describe that which the past never knew, and thereby found a self to be which her precursors never knew to be possible.[7]

I want to insert the caveat that I do not agree with Rorty's interpretation of Nietzsche here; I think Nietzsche knew the fatality of the past as well as anyone and that his self-overcoming was a perfect reconciliation with or affirmation of that fatality. And I want also to point out that Rorty's use of narrative here is much more "postmodern" than either MacIntyre's or Ricoeur's; Rorty's narratives are multiple, ambiguous, and multiteleological.

---

7. Richard Rorty, *Contingency, Irony, and Solidarity* (New York: Cambridge University Press, 1989), p. 29.

But will, in this passage, has its objects not in the present or the future but in the past. The past can be changed, because what the narration of the past narrates is precisely the future in the service of which the past can be transformed. One thing that is certainly lost, and that we are going to see more emphatically lost in the classical pragmatists, is the pastness of the past, which is its fatality. One comfort that the past holds out to us is that it is potentially a place from which our wills can find rest: it's too late to worry about that; you can't do anything about that now. But if Danto and Rorty are right, the past is always something that we are already in the process of doing something about. Now I am not comfortable saying simply that this is false; I too produce "narrative sentences." But my question is this: if we always treat the past as indeterminate and so always potentially an object of the will, can we achieve any reconciliation with the past as something that is past? Can we also lapse into the moment wherein the past as affirmed but not "falsified," not remade in the image of the future, not administered toward ends? I want to be able to *take shelter from my will* in the allowance of the present to lapse into the past, into a realm where it is no longer up to me what happened.

I not only want this, I have it, and so do you. No doubt there are things you regret or despise that you have done or that have happened to you. But to say that such events are always potentially malleable, always potentially the objects of will, is to say that it is always possible to escape your regrets not by making amends or by doing better, but by an act of remaking the past. I have lost some loves in my life that were very important to me. But now to convert "thus it was" to "thus I willed it" in Rorty's sense, what could that mean with regard to those loves? That if I try hard enough I never lost them at all? Or that if I try hard enough I can now want to have lost them, in fact I can now want to have lost them at precisely those moments when I most regretted having lost them? This begins to sound like a full-bore hallucination; it begins to sound not like an affirmation of the past but its wholesale phenomenological destruction. If there are ways that, for example, I can renarrate my pain as something I needed, there are ways that I cannot do that without pretending to destroy precisely that pain. If the formulation of the narrative of my past in the present is something that can to some extent be made over into an object of will in the retrospective construction, I can only go so far in this exercise (as Danto, e.g., is well aware) without losing utterly that material I am narrating and thus becoming someone else, someone who didn't have *that* past. *That* past has now, by an act of will, never happened at all. Maybe that is the prerogative of the genius: to become something else by a sheer act of will, the object of which is the past that no longer exists after its transformation by will. I am not and do not want to be a genius of that kind. And finally I don't see how I could be, don't actually see what that means, don't actually see now what is being narrated or what the act of will in question is. What I want, even as I produce narrative sentences, is to hold onto and maybe affirm the fatality of the past; the past in reverse is inexorable, and I want to be the kind of genius, if this could be a kind of genius, who is ground down by that inexorability and who says as he goes under, "yes." That is the Nietzschean genius.

The traditional opposition, again, is between "scientific" and "narrative" historiography. And it is usually held that while "scientific" historiography does indeed suck the temporality out of history, narrative historiography respects temporality. Ricoeur writes that "the cardinal feature of narrative time" is "its ability to combine in variable proportions the chronological component of the episode and the achronological component of the configuration" (225). In other words, narrative historiography can combine the atemporality of science with the temporality of emplotment. Let us consider this a bit. First of all, a work of narrative historiography does itself take time to unfold; it is not fully spatializable, cannot be fully reproduced as a "timeline," for instance. Narrative in this sense is essentially a principle, first, for the compression of time, as a map is a principle for the compression of space. The map gives a miniaturization in space of space, as the narrative gives a miniaturization in time of time. A map that exactly corresponds to the space mapped (as in one of Borges's fables) is useless, or is itself the space that it maps; an absolutely exhaustive narrative that occupies as much time to traverse as the events it narrates (were such a thing possible) is useless (again Borges: "Funes the Memorious"). This compression is also a mode of comprehension; the compression takes place according to certain principles or standards, and the goal is to render the temporal sequence comprehensible. You can now hold the French Revolution or whatever in your hands, go buy it at the store or check it out of the library. The narrative, again, is a principle sorting for relevance or (if Ricoeur is right) organizing its material teleologically.

But such organization, as a matter of practical fact, can only be retrospective. That is Danto's objection to what he calls "substantive philosophy of history" which wants to show us the teleology not only of various segments of the past, but of the present, as if we were trying to say of what works the people born today are the authors. Danto sees that we cannot write a history of the present in a teleological narrative, in a story. One wonders, in this regard, at Hegel and perhaps MacIntyre. Thus, to locate the present as an historical moment is to regard it retrospectively; it is to engage in a nostalgia for the present moment or to immolate ourselves into the future. That is why it is puzzling to say such things as that we live in narratives; we all know that there can be no nostalgia for the present moment. That is why narrative history cannot be that in which we presently live; that is why, finally, narrative history consumes itself: it consumes its own material in its comprehension of it. What is comprehended is what can never, in fact, occur. Comprehension is a mode of falsification, or, truth is falsity. That is, the "knowledge" that proceeds by grasping its object never grasps *it*, but only grasps its own invention— what it remakes in its compression. To comprehend the world is to miss it; to regard it as something always already finished and in fact as something that was never present at all.

Perhaps the most extreme philosophy of history in this regard—the one that pushes the problem to its end and hence makes it obvious—is provided by pragmatism (and to some extent by the related segments of logical positivism). On some early pragmatist accounts, *every* meaningful assertion is an assertion about the future; that includes assertions such as that I feel funny or that I once loved Brunhilda or that the Orioles won the World Series in 1983. That is because the meaning of any claim is supposed to be identical with its consequences in future experience, including (and this is the bit the positivists battened onto) the processes by which in the future it could be verified. Or as James puts it:

> To attain perfect clearness in our thoughts of an object, then, we need only consider what conceivable effects of a practical kind the object may involve—what sensations to expect from it, and what reactions we must prepare. Our conception of these effects, whether immediate or remote, is then for us the whole of our conception of the object, so far as that conception has positive significance at all.[8]

Then truth, for James, is what bears up under these conditions; what gets verified, pays off in our experience, is expedient to believe, satisfies our purposes, and so on. C.I. Lewis and to some extent John Dewey drew out the implications of this for the meaning of claims about the past, namely that they mean something about the future. To say that this view is implausible is an understatement; it is baldly ludicrous, and Danto has ripped it to shreds as effectively as anyone can rip a philosophical position to shreds.[9]

---

8. William James, "What Pragmatism Means," *Pragmatism* (Indianapolis: Hackett, 1981), p. 26.

9. *Narration and Knowledge*, chapter 4.

So I don't need to rip it to shreds again. What I want to do, rather, is to connect this kind of assertion with the whole philosophical orientation of pragmatism, which I think represents the culmination of teleological rationality in the West. It does so in an unprecedented celebration of technologies for selves and for the world, an unprecedented liquidation of all things into ends. And that is perfectly represented by its implications for the treatment of time: the past and the present are meaningless except in the service of or from the point of view of the future. One need hardly drive home the fact that this is paradoxical, that you can't get time going at all on this basis.

Dewey's question is always how every little thing can be turned to account, how it can be used in a technology of the human and nonhuman world that "subdues" that world to human intelligence. His diagnosis of the human condition when he wrote was that though human inquiry has shifted from a dogmatic religious or magical form to a fallibilist, scientific mode, human institutions have lagged behind, and that once we get everything up to speed social-science-wise, we'll get thoroughly modern and set about remaking the world into a more human and humane place. He thought the main problem with science was that it had been put in the service of outdated values and traditions, and that when science itself and its instrumentalities became the source of our values, everything would make sense. If you think that's a caricature, I could quote literally hundreds of passages to exactly that effect. Here are a few:

> Active experimentation must force the apparent facts of nature into forms different to those in which they familiarly present themselves; and thus make them tell the truth about themselves, as torture may compel an unwilling witness to reveal what he has been concealing.[10]

In *Discipline and Punish* Foucault focuses on torture as a spectacle in which power is inscribed on the body of the condemned for the edification and education of onlookers. But think of torture also as experimentation, as a way that the recalcitrant body can be systematically and technologically altered or turned inside-out in order to extract what it conceals. Now think of that as the first social science, and think of social science and science in general as modes of domination. Think, too, about the claim that nature must be altered by human will to appear in its truth, that no fact should be taken at face value, that

---

10. John Dewey, *Reconstruction in Philosophy* (New York: New American Library, 1950 [1919]), p. 48.

nothing ought to be accepted without first being put to trial by torture. This reveals deep suspicion not about "the facts of nature" but about human episte-mological capacities with regard to those facts.

> [The earth's occurences], being at hand, . . . are also capable of being brought under our hand; they can be manipulated, broken up, resolved into elements which can be managed, combined at will in old and new forms. The net result may be termed, I think, without any great forcing, the substitution of a democracy of individual facts equal in rank for the feudal system of an ordered gradation of gen-eral classes of unequal rank. (70)

This quotation expresses to an extreme degree the essence of teleological ratio-nality and historiographical time as it came to be expressed in industrial tech-nology: the processing or annihilation of recalcitrant objects and events into indefinitely malleable, interchangeable raw materials, a nightmare for the enslavement of persons and the earth by democratic metaphysics. Or as Dewey puts it: "Only indefinite substitution and convertibility regardless of quality ren-der nature manageable. The mechanization of nature is the condition of prac-tical and progressive idealism in action" (74).

> [I]n the degree in which the active conception of knowledge pre-vails, and the environment is regarded as something that has to be changed in order to be truly known, men are imbued with courage, with what may almost be termed an aggressive attitude toward nature. The latter becomes plastic, something to be subjected to human uses. (102)

Now Dewey is perhaps not quite so technocratic as these passages make him appear. First of all, he had a very rich conception of ends as the intelligent creation of values, and though he sometimes talks as if ends were fixed and amounted to subduing the environment, he also believed that ends shift in process. Second, and more importantly to my mind, he had also a very rich conceptions of means, best expressed in *Art as Experience*. In an artistic admin-istration of means, an artistic process, it is precisely a devotion to the means themselves which produces the beauty and expressiveness of the finished artis-tic product. The views about art that I expressed in the previous section owe much to Dewey. And yet this richness is also swallowed into a particularly intense version of the tradition of practical rationality: the claim that we act *for* ends, always, everywhere. "[M]ind, whatever else it may be, is at least an organ for the control of the environment in relation to the ends of the life process" (MW 2:41). These ends amount finally, for Dewey, to an ongoing humaniza-tion of the world and of humanity. The declarations of Dewey's that I quoted above express something utterly central to American pragmatism, something without which many of Dewey's other views make no sense. Pragmatism is defined by its emphasis on consequences, by its constant hankering after ends. Here is Dewey on truth (and of course James and Peirce might be quoted to the same effect, more or less):

> If ideas, meanings, conceptions, notions, theories, systems are instrumental to an active reorganization of the given environment, then the test of their validity and value lies in their accomplishing this work. If they succeed in their office, they are reliable, sound, valid, good, true. . . . Confirmation, corroboration, verification lie in works, consequences. Handsome is that handsome does. By their fruits shall ye know them. (128)

Now this is a technological conception of truth. What it means for Dewey is very simple: whatever lets us "reorganize" our environment coherently is true. I think the pragmatic theory of truth is false (more or less obviously false), and I think it is dangerous. To quote myself: truth crushes, truth kills, but it rarely works. That the pragmatic theory of truth was developed at the high-water mark of industrial capitalism is no coincidence. To say that is to perform a genealogy of Dewey, and Dewey is himself one of the great innovators of the genealogical method. But it must be said that unlike the genealogies of Nietzsche or Foucault, Dewey's is marked by a teleological optimism that would be charming if it weren't so scary. Everything, for Dewey, is progressing toward the liquidation of the environment by machinery for the sake of human reconstruction; everything has been tending that way since the Greeks; now we approach the millennium. The science and technology that Dewey celebrates are instruments of domination, and they have helped "us" dominate other cultures. But they are also modes of self-construction whereby "we" make "ourselves" what "we" take "ourselves" to be: "intelligent" and "powerful" and "human."

It is worth remarking on another difference between Dewey's genealogy and Nietzsche's or Foucault's: whereas the latter are about the past, for the former there are no sentences strictly speaking about the past, a genealogy for Dewey or Lewis could only be some sort of prediction or guide about or for future experiences. So if he's telling a story about the Greeks or whatever, it's a prediction about the further course of our experiences, and to say it is true would be to say something like that it will enrich our future experiences. That is, the apparent references to the past are, by Dewey's own account, resources for the future; "reconstruction" in this sense, we might say, remakes the past into the future; or rather, since we can't actually be meaning anything about the past, it vaporizes the past into the future. Danto is concerned to show—what is trivial on his view that historiography tries to say truths about the past, and what is pretty clear on the face of it anyway—that this is going to make a hash out of history. But I'm more concerned now with what Dewey's view entails about the "meaning" or the "truth" of the present. I suppose that the claim that I'm in pain, e.g., would be a sort of prediction: if it works in guiding my future experience, it's true; and it means precisely this guiding. That has a certain plausibility; the meaning of *pain* in that sense is the subsequent dose of morphine or the motivation for it. But again in this philosophy, the present has no presence. There's no silence, no emptiness, no ecstasy, only the endless chatter that comes at us from the wraith-realm of what has not yet occurred.

Dewey has his own narrative of Western intellectual history. He writes:

> The savage takes things "as they are," and by using caves and roots and occasional pools leads a meager and precarious existence. The civilized man goes to distant mountains and dams streams. He builds reservoirs, digs channels, and conducts the waters to what had been a desert. He searches the world to find plants and animals that will thrive. He takes native plants and by selection and cross-fertilization improves them. He introduces machinery to till the soil and care for the harvest. By such means he may succeed in making the wilderness bloom like a rose. (82)

Or like Los Angeles. We are now in the happy condition of having dammed every major river in the continental United States.

Now to call folks who take things as they are "savages" is precisely to extrude them from the narrative of progress that Dewey gives us. (Keep in mind that this narrative of progress is, all of it, about the future. Dewey has "pragmatic" reasons for telling us this narrative; what it means for the narrative to be true "about the past" is precisely to guide us toward some future.) If we can understand ourselves as powerful and able to control our environment, it is because we can understand the "savage" as degraded by the necessity of adapting to conditions without engaging adequately in transformation. Our forms of power are associated by us with "mind" or "intelligence" and with our dominance of "history" as a teleological narrative. The savage is what does not appear in history except as its limit or its exterior or the primal muck from which history emerged. Savages cannot have a history, for one thing, because they are supposed to be illiterate and their cultures unrecorded, not coagulated in an archive which would allow our hypotheses "about" their past to be tested in future research experiences. This series of ejections has little to do with them; it is a way we make ourselves ourselves or try to convince ourselves of who we are. But this exclusion is fatal as well, because it freezes the "tradition" in isolation from the conditions of its own production, from the little zones where it is capable of being compromised and hence of becoming, and from the exterior zones that lend it shape. "The Western tradition" is dead because it seeks to extrude from itself all signs of life by an ejected asceticism. This is particularly true in the academic discourse where "the canon" actually gets constructed these days; our prose is dead, our bodies are inessential, our tradition so serious that it hurts even to contemplate it.

Inquiry, which is, of course, a central human activity for Dewey, is "the controlled or directed transformation of an indeterminate situation into one that is so determinate in its constituent distinctions and relations as to convert the elements of the original situation into a unified whole" (*Logic*, LW 12:108). What I am asking about is the value and even the possibility of such unifications: why do we need them, how are they produced, and how, if need be, can we get out of them? I'd like to recommend a dose of disunity, disproportion, and derangement—derangement of the good, of inquiry, and of life. I'd like to recommend letting go of the obsessive creation of meanings, the obsessive holding up of the world to a tribunal of the human. I'd like to recommend the arts of acceptance and revile the arts of control. I'd like to see us break down, as a culture and as subjects. Or rather, I'd like us to see what in ourselves and our cultures exceeds meanings, what is already deranged: the ways we have already broken down or have never been put together. And I would like to learn to live in that and with that, and to celebrate it.

In pragmatism, rationality has gotten so intense that life is never yet being experienced. All meanings are held in reserve, at the disposal of the future. If there could be any time in such a structure, it would be a pure resource—so much coal to be stripmined. But here even the narrative becomes impossible; here time is "permanently" deferred, and nothing is ever happening now (from which we might as well go ahead and draw the conclusion that nothing ever happens at all). Or rather, if there can be narratives according to this philosophy, they cannot do anything like what Ricoeur or MacIntyre want them to do; they cannot connect us to our tradition if we are considering our tradition as something with a past, and they cannot "coordinate" the past with the future by emplotment. What they could do, I guess, is provide us with more future; they could rearticulate the future. All meanings, recall, are consequences. Every assertion is about the future, which is actually comedic: it turns out that what I have forgotten is *the future*; my nostalgia is for *the future*, and so forth. Well, that is a good result at least in this sense: it *enables* me to forget the future *in* the future (not in the present, since "the present" means something about the future), so that I can overcome practical rationality insofar as I am not omniscient.

Deleuze and Guattari say that to become is to deviate from a model. And now I'd like to introduce *becoming* explicitly as a technical term: becoming is change in ateleological time. And I am going to put my prepostmodernist or postpostmodernist cards on the table: I think this is real time, not an aspect of phenomenology. I think this is the time of nature, which changes, but not purposively. And just to put all the cards down: I think that everything that happens in the universe and to human beings happens by becoming in this sense, I think project and its comprehension are a delusion. The model or standard is articulated as a telos; it is an ambition. One cultivates the goal of a perfect normalization or reconciliation to the standard. One strives for perfect whiteness, perfect heterosexuality, and so on. (Deleuze and Guattari remark that even women become woman in this sense: that their womanliness is itself a deviation from the standard.) That progress toward the standard would be a becoming, if becoming simply meant change, though here too change would be dependent on deviation, in this case antecedent to the achievement of the standard. But to change away from the standard, to become in deviation, is, first of all, to transgress. So for a white guy (and assuming for the time being that such things are possible) becoming a woman is a transgression, becoming a black person is a transgression, becoming a homosexual is a transgression, burning all my money is a transgression, and so on. It follows, second, that becoming would then be a shift out of or a move away from the teleology in which the dominant narrative or standard is articulated. (Of course, and to repeat, I am not denying that this process could then be narrated.) This is a shift also out of the standing time in which the present is deferred into a future, or in which time is projected spatially onto a map with a big X on it somewhere. Ricoeur, with regard to "scientific" history: "A secret dream of emulating the cartographer or the diamond cutter animates the historical enterprise" (176).

The odd thing about the view I'm developing is that it appears to allow that there are changes that are not becomings, changes instituted in the self-annihilating or standing time of the dominant narrative. To acknowledge that would be to acknowledge that time can indeed be ordered teleologically, at least locally and to some extent. But what I am interested in here is the possibility of the moment, nested in the postmodern multiplication of narratives, identities, minorities, in which the narrative collapses into an experience of utter or sheer becoming, for the multiplication of narratives provides the vertiginous moment of sacrificial transgression or the slow absorption into ceremonial time. The fact is that one tumbles in this process out of the standard and into the elsewhere, and this tumble is always potentially narratable as the interruption of the standard's teleology; it is usually possible at this point for the standing time to be reinstated. That is the structure of "slumming": I become black or become gay for an evening; the next day I'm back at work in the white-guy world. In fact the danger of finding these zones of transgression (transgression *for me*, qua white guy) and of becoming into them is really the worst and ultimate danger (as these things go): the reappropriation of the "minority," its smooth integration into the standard narrative and standing time. Slumming renders becoming narratable.

And here I return painfully to the shortcomings of multiculturalism and postmodernism, painfully because believe me I feel their allure and experience their salutary moments. Postmodernism and multiculturalism multiply narrative locations, hence possibilities of transgression and becoming. But they are administered in academic institutions, and they return these zones to the standard or bring them into the standard, even as they may also to some extent rearticulate the standard. One eliminates talk of, say the "primitive" or the "savage" as that which exists in preteleological time: but one does this precisely in order to bring the previously primitive and savage into history, to write a history of them in relation to us. One enters them in historiographical standing time, into the archive. It is all very well for Deleuze and Guattari to talk about becoming-minority. But they need (or needed) to think also, first, of the limits of this becoming for the white man. They needed to think seriously about the effects of white guys "becoming" black on black people, or rather, how laughable the idea of a white guy becoming black is to black people. Keep in mind that the "black" location as delineated from within the standard is a sheer limit condition: we're minds, they're bodies, and so on. So that to "leave" the suburb for the slum for the evening is not at all to leave the suburb; to conceive the slum as the transgression that liberates is to conceive the standard again as standard. To assert, for example, a "women's history" is at once to seek power and to enter into the standing time in which existence is deferred indefinitely.

These locations are not exhausted by our use of them or definition of them as transgressions or as becomings; these are real cultural locations as well as imaginary limit-conditions. There are meanings of being African that are much more than the imaginary meanings of not being European. But we white guys need to think with extreme seriousness about what sort of access we could have to those meanings, and what we want that access for. Of course, we want this access as an expression of and treatment for our self-loathings and the oppressions we commit, which is to say that we want them as ways out of standing time and out of our narratives, that is, we'd like to take a break—need to. And "others" can provide us with the sensations of such an egress. But if they are to provide anything more than that, anything more than the narratable transgressions of the safari and the night out in Harlem, then they require at a minimum roughly a lifetime of total immersion. It is all very well to talk flippantly about my becoming woman, but I need to think pretty seriously about what that could actually mean.

> Order-words bring immediate death to those who receive the order, or potential death if they do not obey, or a death they must themselves inflict, take elsewhere. A father's orders to his son, "You will do this," "You will not do that," cannot be separated from the little death sentence the son experiences on the point of his person. Death, death: it is the only judgment, and it is what makes judgment a system. The verdict. *But the order-word is also something else*, inseparably connected: it is like a warning cry or a message to flee. It would be oversimplifying to say that flight is a reaction against the order-word; rather, it is included in it, as its other face in a complex assemblage, its other component. Canetti is right to invoke the lion's roar, which enunciates flight and death simultaneously. (ATP 107)

The one order-word that subsumes all the rest is *end*: the teleology you've failed in, the moment after the moment of surcease, the reconciliation of the transgressor to the law, the return of the prodigal; reaffirmation, reincarnation, the conquest of death, the project sufficient for an entire life that cannot end at death. The moment of sacrifice, the entrance to the slum, the sex-change, the absolutely unremarkable, brought again face to face with the death that awaits it and then what lurks behind death. The self-immolation narrated, the living death, the afterlife. If we find a way away, it will not be away, nor a way.

CHAPTER FOUR

PRESENCE AND FATE

I

The first part of this chapter is going to be about the precisionist still-life painting that flourished around Philadelphia in the late nineteenth century. I'm
writing about this sort of painting, the great practitioners of which include
William Harnett, John Peto, John Haberle, George Cope, and Jefferson David
Chalfant, first because I love it and second because I think it has remarkable
implications for the treatment of time and representation. Also, this discussion
will have the virtue of giving us a little break from textual interpretation; consider it a touching expression of hope that the hegemony of language can be
compromised, and that maybe that hegemony does not extend fully to images.

First, a bit of background. All of these painters, with the exception of
Haberle, who lived in New Haven, were in one way or another connected with
the Pennsylvania Academy of Fine Arts, and it is probable that they were all
affected by the example of Thomas Eakins, who taught there in the 1870s.
Eakins's aesthetic extruded every element besides truth to the world as a distraction, and many of his brutally frank portraits (which are among the greatest masterpieces of that art in history, comparable to Rembrandt and Hals) were
rejected by their sitters because Eakins refused all idealization. Harnett and Peto
painted almost no portraits, indeed almost no paintings at all that are not still
life broadly conceived. They specialized in modest but beautifully rendered
table-top arrangements of books, pipes, mugs, and musical instruments, and also
in illusionistic scenes of objects hung on walls or doors, such as letter racks,

signs, currency, and hunting trophies. Harnett certainly set the basic themes and methods for the style, which was very similar to Dutch seventeenth-century still life and in particular to the trompe-l'oeil school of Cornelis Gysbrechts. Harnett's work is almost unbelievable in its precision of rendering and its bravura displays of illumination and foreshortening. Indeed, the sheets of music that he painted can actually be read, and many of the newspapers and other textual materials he displayed can be made out word for word using a magnifying glass. Typical of his output is "My Gems," located in the National Gallery in Washington. It depicts, on a table top, a Dutch-style beer stein, a lamp, a flute, sheet music, ink well and quill, books including Dante's *Purgatorio*, a lamp, a pipe, ashes, and burned out matches. The light is oblique and raking in a manner reminiscent of Caravaggio; it picks out highlights and heightens the sense of three dimensions as the objects sink into the mysterious chiaroscuro background. Often in Harnett's pictures there is a live coal in the pipe and wisps of smoke rising.

Peto was a friend of Harnett's and in some ways obviously derivative. Virtually all his themes were developed first by Harnett, though Peto often explored them more deeply. But in other ways their styles were quite different. Peto is not, like Harnett, basically concerned to make the viewer gasp at the palpability and detail of his renderings or to approach the canvas and try to peel off bits of newspaper. (Harnett's work often had to be put behind rails or guarded. One version of his *After the Hunt* hung in Stewart's saloon in New York City; it was the subject of various wagers over whether the objects were painted or real. Indeed, I overheard a tour guide at the Brandywine River Museum in Chadds Ford, Pennsylvania, telling her little knot of patrons that DeScott Evans's *Free Sample—Try One*, a picture of almonds behind broken glass, another version of which hangs in the Pennsylvania Academy of Fine Arts, had to be placed behind plexiglas because people kept touching it.) Peto uses a much smoother, flatter finish and renders much less detail. He uses illusion as a theme rather than actually trying to achieve it; very few of Peto's canvases are finished to the extent that they manifest any serious illusionistic intent. Rather, they are often reminiscent of pure abstraction: they play with form. The apotheosis of this aspect of Peto's work is *Letter Rack on Black Door* from 1895, which reduces its already fundamentally two-dimensional theme to rectangles of intense color. In addition, there is a distinctive emotional flavor in Peto's work. While Harnett, I would say, is charming, urbane, and maybe bourgeois, and where the artist's sensibility is effaced, or where that sensibility is present precisely as an effacement of sensibility in favor of the object itself, Peto is seedy, melancholy; every item he depicts is worn or broken, and his work is much more pointedly introspective and autobiographical than Harnett's. Peto recorded his life in inanimate artifacts; one almost wants to say, he recorded his life as an inanimate artifact. His life is embodied in trompe l'oeil depictions of letters to and from the painter, pictures of persons he loved, his pipes and kitchen utensils, and so on. That is, his life is present in its effects, particularly in the effects of long use and consequent wear on the objects he depicts; he shows the inanimate traces of a life—its effects on its environment—*as* his life. Hence, the life Peto depicts is a life in fusion with its artifactual environment, a life in which there is no deep distinction between person and thing.

An excellent comparison can be made at the Brandywine, where a painting by Harnett and one by Peto depict almost identical themes: pipe, mug, and biscuits. Where Harnett suggests the texture of the mug with impasto and captures the smoldering pipe with a wizardly display of detail, Peto focuses on pure flat forms with almost no internal delineation. And where the emotional tone of the Harnett, if any, emerges only out of the objects he depicts and the devotion with which he depicts them, Peto carries an emotional intensity into his treatment of the objects. That is, for Harnett, the expression is presented as inherent in the objects—their selection and arrangement, and the devotion, amounting almost to religious fervor, with which they are painted. Harnett makes a sacrament of the ordinary artifact, and he makes the painting into a self-effacement before the world—a prayer before the world or an offering to the world from the world. For Peto, on the other hand, the depicted object is, first of all, already invested with emotion by the modalities of its use, and the painting takes on an independent status as itself a simplification and abstraction of the real object and hence an object with its own expressive capacities. This feature is emphasized by the fact that many Petos are unfinished (perhaps intentionally in some cases) and the fact that they're not all in the best of shape, having spent decades in attics and so forth. Harnetts, on the other hand, are invariably finished perfectly, utterly: everything is as nailed down as it ever gets in painting.

A Haberle also hangs at Chadd's Ford, and it is hilarious: *Torn in Transit*, a theme he returned to several times. It is a painting of a painting that has been wrapped in brown paper and tied with a string and to which mailing labels have been affixed. But the paper has been torn away, revealing a grandiose, almost fantastic landscape of the sort favored by Bierstadt or Cole. The signature is a return address: "From Haberle." The painting is a wonderful puncturing of pretensions. It collapses the grand scenery (which is not, by the way, that much less well painted than a Cole) into a flat still-life element; it is about the illusion of illusion, or the illusion of recession in space on a flat canvas. And it renders Cole's cosmic ambitions into a modest element of a still-life joke. It brings the grand aesthetic gesture and hence the pretensions of aesthetic connoisseurship smack up against the picture plain and smack up against the artist's ridicule. In a pair of ink sketches, *Trees By a Stream* and *Trompe L'oeil With Bird*, he works a similar commentary on representation. The former is a naturalistic landscape, unremarkable enough; the latter takes the very same landcape sketch and shows it (in trompe l'oeil) curling at the edges, and then, just for the hell of it, drops a couple of other pictures in amongst the trees, supported apparently by the branches. This might as well be Magritte. Haberle is probably best known for his paintings of currency. In one famous case, Haberle painted a newspaper clipping headlined "John Haberle the Counterfeiter" next to a precisionist rendering of a ten dollar bill. A favorite subject was the warning against reproduction that appeared on the back of nineteenth-century paper money. (Indeed, Harnett was actually arrested for counterfeiting and Haberle and Peto threatened with prosecution if they did not cease painting cash.) Almost everything Haberle painted embodied this sort of nested joking commentary on representational practices; in some sense he was the first postmodern artist. In fact, alone of all these artists he concentrated almost wholly (at least for the most active decade and a half of his artistic career) on pure trompe l'oeil that made a serious attempt to deceive. A typical work is *The Changes of Time,* an anthologistic extravaganza of deceptive effects, including a history of American paper money, a newspaper clipping under a cracked magifying glass, a fake frame (depicting all the Presidents of the United States in fake relief) and so on. He was perhaps even more obsessive in his rendering than Harnett: his finishes are perfectly flat and his brushwork completely invisible.

Where Harnett, Peto, and Haberle devoted more or less their whole careers to these limited subjects, Cope and Chalfant hopped on the bandwagon when it became clear that there was a market for such paintings. Cope's treatments of Buffalo Bill's outfits and hunting paraphernalia apply Harnett's techniques to Western themes with admirable craft. In a very unusual composition, also at the Brandywine River Museum, he depicts Indian artifacts, including arrowheads, beadwork, and peace pipes, on a board along with a bowie knife and a pistol. There is a target on the board with bullet holes and the marks of a thrown knife in it. In some sense this work is a history of the contact and conflict of European and Native America. The wood grain is rendered with consummate skill. In general, Cope favored a paler palette and more pointed themes than Harnett and Peto. Like them, he also worked on tabletop compositions, which, like Harnett's, are perfectly finished (though not always in correct perspective), but which display less cluttered arrangements of objects.

Chalfant's work in this vein is among the most ravishingly beautiful and most ruthlessly simplified painting that can be found in any style of the period in Europe or the Americas. Both Harnett and Peto painted violins hanging on walls many times. But Chalfant's treatment, an example of which is in the collection of the Metropolitan Museum, renders the violin in loving detail on an almost plain white background. This both increases the illusionistic possibilities and eliminates all distractions from the perfection of the rendering. Where Harnett's musical instruments were often treated as emblems (as in *Music and Good Luck* at the Met, which pairs violin with horseshoe in a nice but very self-conscious arrangement and with considerable clutter), Chalfant's violin is absolutely simply itself; it is lovely because it doesn't *signify*, it simply *is*. Chalfant's still lifes are characterized by a sense of serenity that emerges from the process of eliminating the extraneous. (Miles Davis: "I always listen for what I can leave out.")

In their own time, these works were commercial. They generally hung in store windows, newspaper offices, and bars, where many of them actually served as advertisements. Peto's letter racks, for example, often included the depiction of ads for the establishment in which they were hung, photographic portraits of the owners, bits of the relevant newspaper, and so forth. For the most part, these works were anything but high art and were intended to amaze and amuse. The "aesthetic" effect, if any, emerged only later, and emerged out of the devotion to the worldly objects depicted. But more important was the playfulness with which these paintings sought to achieve illlusionistic effects (or played even with *that*) and the sheer Barnum-like sideshow atmosphere.

Alright. This tradition is relevant to our present concerns in a variety of ways. First of all, it is a narrative art in some sense. Harnett and Peto in particular painted the story of their lives in objects: the books they loved, the musical instruments they played (Peto was an accomplished musician), the pipes they smoked, the food they ate: the objects accumulated and used over the course of a lifetime, all of them showing ravages of time or consecration and personalization by use. When Peto wanted to paint a "portrait" of his daughter, for instance, he painted a worn photograph of her tacked to a wall from which the green paint is peeling, with his initials carved into the wood and the year "1901" as a graffito. Harnett has a delightful painting called "The Social Club" which is a gathering of pipes on a marble shelf in which the characters are delineated by the nature of their pipes, or in which the pipes themselves are characters.

So again, it is not false to say that these paintings recount stories. But they do so by an absolute crystallization of a single moment in the story. That is, first

of all, due to the sheer fact that they are paintings and not works of, say, popular or amusing literature, they do not unfold over time. At every moment in
which it is present, a painting—that particular physical object—is fully present,
present all at once, and in the case of these paintings, can be surveyed in an
instant. Where a story or a drama coordinates the reader's or theatre-goer's time
into the represented time by compression, a painting concretizes a moment in
time. But there are paintings that are devoted to suggesting what has gone
before and what will come after, that show a moment in an ongoing temporal
flow wrapped into a narrative structure. That is the nature of "history" painting, for example.

On the other hand, the still life in general is, precisely, still. It does not
suggest a moment arrested in furious or significant action, but rather a repose
or equipoise achieved at a particular moment. And this effect is at its most
intense in an "illusonistic" still life of the type we are considering. Indeed, the
illusionistic effect is "instantaneous": if you are caught by the illusion, you are
caught momentarily; as soon as you begin to move, think, or inspect, the illusion is punctured, and the moment at which it is punctured is the moment
when, as intended, you come to appreciate the artist's craft. So whereas a grand
sweeping history painting crystallizes a moment for the purpose of conveying
a teleological flow, a Peto arrests a flow for the purpose of conveying a crystalline moment. The items are, first of all, arranged and, second of all, worn:
they show the "signs" of age, of constant use; they trace an autobiography. But
if Peto's work constitutes an autobiography, it does so by a serial arrest of time,
a constant collapsing of the life back into its embodiment, at each moment, *as*
that moment.

These paintings embody a "theory" of time, but it is an antiteleological
ordering in which nothing, not even the past, escapes the gravitational field of
the present. These works of consummate craft deliver a theory of the time of
craft in which the future as well as the past is held in the service of the present,
in which all the time encompassed is crystallized into total presence. Where the
history painting places the moment at the service of the narrative, Peto places
the narrative at the service of the moment. The narrative is present only in that
and insofar as it finds reality in perfect presence. Your sudden sense of the reality both of the depiction and what it depicts shows that what is real now is
what is real *now*.

Nevertheless, the past is present in these works as it is caught up in and
rendered into presence. The painting is like "the kiss at the end of a fist" (Chan-
dler); the painting is a blow: it concretizes the "movement" out of the past into
the future as the slap that wakes you into presence. A punch proceeds by an act

of will: the arm coils, lashes; it is an event, a temporal smear. But the blow delivered is instantaneous and hence devastating; it collapses your consciousness out of history. The painting is like a blow: it wraps up a conflicted past, resolves it into the violent present, sends it again careening on its way. There is nostalgia all over these paintings; they were nostalgic even when they were painted, and now they are pleasing for the fact that they look like antiques, that they depict with devoted realism items that would now be antiques. It is impossible to achieve in the past a nostalgia for the past, by which I mean to say there is never nostalgia for the present. Nostalgia brings you to presence as emerging out of a particular past: the melancholy of unrecoverability, of being powerless before time or broken by it, of experiencing yourself as irreversible, of necessarily being where you are, of being struck now by the past in its fatality, by the fact that it is, contra Rorty, no longer an object of will.

Cope's *Indian Relics* is a history painting; in fact, it is almost unique in this regard. There are few still-life history paintings in Western art; certainly there are few that survey a couple of centuries. But first, as is not the case in a history painting that depicts persons, the depicted items are inanimate; they can't move themselves around. They don't gesticulate, they aren't in the middle of anything, they are just there. Paintings themselves are inanimate objects; they are fully there at every moment they are there; they're never in the middle of anything, never getting something accomplished, never aiming to achieve anything. These paintings celebrate that fact in the illusionistic effect. But then, the still-life elements themselves aren't in the middle of anything either; they have a past (and indeed, the items in Cope's painting are museum-like; they are meant precisely to "capture" the past and to inform us about it), but they are fully present when they are present. The "museum-like" quality of the Cope, however, is punctured precisely by its alternate character as a target: the panel is penetrated by bullet holes. Here, the "preservation" of the past that is characteristic of the museum is contrasted with the explosion of the gunshot that penetrates and splinters the museum piece.

We might say that just as present existence cannot be deferred until a future time, the past cannot be preserved. The narrative practices that have goal as their goal, that is, that seek to defer or delay the present moment or to wrap it or annihilate it into the future, have their correlate in the "museum" practice that seeks to "preserve" the past or to allow what is past to transcend its pastness and emerge into presence now. The past has not, however, been preserved, and the present cannot be preserved into the future. Such practices seek to reduce all presents to futures, seek to dessicate all presents. The goal of the project is its own annihilation. The practice of preservation seeks to hold the present, but not *as* present: in seeking to *possess* the present, to make of the present an enduring possession, it must precisely remove it from presence, and, like the project, perish in a loss of its own material. Here we might think of the practices of the family snapshot or the family video tape; we're trying to record and preserve the present moment, and of course the present moment is what cannot be recorded or preserved, and the practices by which we seek to do this are also practices in which we try to achieve absence in the present, that is, to defer presence until a later time, when we can sit down to watch the video. We're not there having the experience, we're behind the camera both distancing ourselves from the present and preserving it. That distance is a release and an amusement. But of course it is obviously paradoxical: what it could possibly mean to distance yourself from the present is a complete mystery. The practices that seek to achieve this distance are practices of *ownership* and hence of power. To try to preserve the present in the video is to claim ownership of the present, to treat the present as a possession—to try, for one thing, to render the temporal spatial so that it can be owned and to make it into the photograph, the photo album, the videotape. To "preserve" the present is to seek power over it, which is always to remove its presence, because the present, if anything, always owns *us*. We are *its* playthings; we are powerless before it; we exist inside it at all times, at its whim, so to speak—in its whim, like Job in the whim of God.

So we are in fact inanimate objects. We exist fully in the presence of the present at every moment in which we do exist. (This is like one of Zeno's paradoxes: the arrow in flight occupies at each moment an area precisely equal to its size; therefore it does not move. Harnett's paintings are illustrations of this argument.) The present cannot be preserved, and the past has not been preserved, and the present cannot be deferred, and time cannot be possessed, and time cannot be rendered over into a commodity (though in fact in our economy we are always purporting to buy and sell it in its embodiment as labor), and time cannot be spatialized. We are still-life elements: even the grand tableaux of great men performing actions of immense historical significance (taking the Tennis Court oath, crossing the Delaware) are still lifes. They are inanimate objects. They preserve nothing. They can be bought and sold, but to buy and sell them is not to buy and sell the history they depict or even to buy and sell the history of the history painting. That is the message, too, of the illusionistic effect which calls you out of the historical significance of the item you are surveying into the presence of the experience you are now having; the items in the Cope have been "preserved" as in a museum display, and the Cope itself is in a museum collection. The preservations are nested, layered so that we get an archeology in which we can excavate the strata of time. But this time is "preserved" only to have that preservation splintered or riddled with bullets in the illusionistic effect that makes us aware that we are experiencing right now what is present right now. That is, of course, a perfectly trivial or tautological realization, which only serves to emphasize the difficulties inherent in any of its alternatives.

That is the flip side of MacIntyre and Ricoeur's centralization of narrative: they're (purportedly) living for the future, but they're (purportedly) living *in* the past; both men are above all "historians of ideas" and are caught in the dialectic of nostalgia. Their particular nostalgia is for the meganarratives of the future made long in the past: the Aristotelian, the Augustinian, and so on. Their project is the narrativization of life, bringing a teleology to bear on life, but this project is nostalgic in the sense that it seeks a preservation of the past, and so can only be happening in whatever present they are writing in. What is preserved is only what is no longer present; what is preserved, that is, held through time, held into "our own" time for the sake of the future, is only what time has already immolated. In seeking to grasp and reinstitute these narratives, they show only that these narratives have already annihilated themselves, that insofar as they were successful at all, they brought about their own ends. In that sense the narrative nostalgia of MacIntyre and Ricoeur is perfectly poised opposite the representational practices of Harnett and Peto in which that annihilation is acknowledged perfectly, effortlessly, in which the presence of the past is always completely wrapped into the presence of the present, in which the pastness of the past is both acknowledged and mourned, in which its annihilation is formulated in the present into an experience of perfect presence. Like MacIntyre and Ricoeur, Harnett and Peto ache for the past. But the fact that this ache is happening in the present is not effaced; there is not in these paintings an immersion in the past that seeks to leave the present and enter the past. And of course there can be no ache for the past where the experience of the presence of the present is not extremely poignant. (There is a sense in MacIntyre's work, for example, that he feels himself to be displaced in time.) That poignancy is what Harnett and Peto acknowledge by making ache the emotion that informs the present crystallized experience. In both MacIntyre/Ricoeur and Harnett/Peto a *love* for the past is expressed. But in the books this love takes the form of an attempt at time travel: one wants to return to the past or to possess the past. In the paintings this love is intensified by being acknowledged to occur in the artists' present. The fact that the object of love cannot be held or preserved is acknowledged in the very act that holds dear the past.

This reversal of field is going to be characteristic of my treatment of other aspects of these paintings. First of all, with the possible exception of postmodern art, the Philly still-life tradition makes the most elaborate use of text in the history of art. There is text in almost every painting: addressed letters, newspapers, books, packing labels, calling cards, written music, marked boxes, advertisements, graffitti, and so on. That is a good subject for trompe l'oeil effects because the text is basically flat, so that a flat depiction could be fairly easily mistaken for the real thing (nor is it quite inaccurate to say that a precisionistically rendered text is itself a text, that it both depicts something and is what it depicts). And painting print is a good way, further, to play with the various possibilities of dimensionality: paper is fairly flat, but to depict it as rolled, torn, curled, or cracked with age displays its disintegration (a key theme especially of Peto's work) and makes the flat object more illusionistic by "popping" it into three dimensions. Of course the illusionistic effect is an *effect*; the surface itself that encompasses the text as it pops out into the viewer's space is two-dimensional (or roughly two-dimensional, in the case of Harnett's impasto passages). So you take a flat object and depict it displayed in three dimensions as the depiction itself remains two-dimensional; once the nature of the thing is appreciated, it "wavers" between being seen as flat, as three-dimensional, then as flat again in a different way. And painting print is also in general a perfect subject for a display of virtuoso painting on two levels: first, if you can perfectly imitate the writing on a bank note, much less a paragraph or two of newsprint, you're a serious crafter. Second, if you can *suggest*, say, a column of newsprint by what is in fact just some smudges of paint, then you are a magician or con man of the sort that all these guys delighted in being. You get people to approach and *try* to read what is in fact not a text at all. The former is Harnett's and Haberle's basic strategy, the latter Peto's; in fact, unlike even Harnett, Haberle's scraps of newspaper are always legible, and are usually reviews praising the artist; that gives him the opportunity for editing. The delightful Alfred Frankenstein points out that in the review depicted in *The Changes of Time*, he's edited out the words "without being in any sense a work of art."[1]

More significantly for present purposes, these paintings reduce text to picture; they reduce or expand the textual element into a pictorial element and cross-pollinate the representational modes, but always for the sake of the picture, always in the picture, always under the aegis of pictoricity. This can be seen most easily in the practice of all of these painters of trivializing, fragmenting,

---

1. Alfred Frankenstein, *The Reality of Appearance: The Trompe L'oeil Tradition in American Painting* (New York: New York Graphic Society, 1970), p. 114.

and destroying textual materials. It's a pretty stupid exercise to try to read one of Harnett's newspapers: for one thing they are usually upside down, and standing on your head in a museum (where most of these things are now, unfortunately, mostly in storage) is acutely embarrassing, as I know by traumatic experience. Furthermore, the papers are rolled or folded, so at best you get disconnected bits that you are left trying to decode. Usually, having done so (and apart from the case of Haberle's newspaper clippings about himself), you realize that they're simply trivial or unconnected with the rest of the picture; you realize that you have been tricked into seeking significance where the point is the lack of significance even of text, the paradigmatically significant object. Haberle played with this as well in his completely trivial messages on trompe l'oeil chalk boards, for example. In *The Changes of Time* he actually depicts a letter sticking out of an addressed envelope in which we cannot read the writing but can tell that it's reversed, that is, that we are looking through the paper at writing on the other side. Then you realize that the basic order of the picture in question is not the order of the sign at all, that the sign has been divested of its meaning by being made over into a still-life element even in cases where it is legible. Furthermore, Peto in particular rips texts apart constantly; hardly one of his board paintings does not feature the tacked corners of a card or clipping that has been torn from the wall. He is actually violent with regard to text; he seeks its annihilation, in which only its unprinted corners remain. Or maybe he leaves us a few letters or superimposes textual bits over each other in a letter rack so that they can't be read. Again, he shows us texts in physical embodiment, concealment, and disintegration, where their most obvious property is their lack of meaning; they are things that should mean but don't. Quickly or slowly in Peto, texts are in the process of being compromised in their legibility, in their sense.

This practice displays the dependence of the text on its physical "manifestation" or "expression" (inscription) in order for it to function textually at all. The sovereign or "abstract" word, higher than the picture (according to Plato or Hegel, e.g.) precisely because of its distance from the physical or in its alleged abstraction from the conditions of human perception, now is displayed as a picture in its universal dependence as a communicative instrument on the concrete physical manifestation. In the ontology of the text, the "same" text can appear now here, now there: Dante's *Purgatorio* is not identical with the particular copy that Harnett owned; it's everywhere there's a copy, that is, nowhere in particular. Thus it participates in the construction of "reason" as an abstracted faculty or "master" of the body; it is the object of the highest human activity on Aristotle's account: study.

> The best is understanding, or whatever else seems to be the natural
> ruler and leader, and to understand what is fine and divine, by being
> itself either divine or the most divine element in us. Hence com-
> plete happiness will be its activity expressing its proper virtue; and
> we have said that this activity is the activity of study. (*Nicomachean
> Ethics*, 13.3)

And again: "Such a life would be superior to the human level. For someone
will live it not in so far as he is a human being, but insofar as he has some
divine element in him" (13.37). Text is the proper object for study in this
regard just because it seems to occupy some ontological status that is not
merely physical or not merely particular, and by participating in that status
through study we ourselves come to be little gods; we transcend the physical
and the particular. This is in turn associated with power; it is this faculty that
is the highest, that should rule both the self and the state. But Harnett and Peto
deconstruct such a view by displaying the complete dependence of the text
on its physical inscription. They reduce or ridicule the "power" of the text and
hence also the power of the "mind" conceived as Aristotle conceives it, and
they do this to make possible a sensual pleasure not only in pipes or violins
but in language. For example, Haberle's work always features elaborate puns
embodied into depicted texts in newspaper clippings, carved graffiti, or
inscriptions, as in *Time and Eternity*, a kind of parody *Vanitas* featuring a watch
juxtaposed with a cross. The scrap of newspaper is datelined "Providence." And
of course this sort of painting was dismissed in its own time as "mindless" and
excluded from the salons, even while it was being enjoyed in the saloons. This
is, as well, the meaning in Harnett of the effacement of the maker: the resolution not to make a world out of mind or to impose the order of the text onto
the antecedent reality.

Contemporary art and aesthetics have often sought to "textualize" pictures; that couldn't be clearer, for example, than in Goodman's *Languages of
Art*—perhaps the preeminent work in "analytic aesthetics"—which argues that
pictures ought to be understood as texts, picture systems as languages. And as
Tom Wolfe argues in *The Painted Word*, much modern and postmodern art is
incomprehensible without its accompanying linguistic explanations, a fact
which he condemns but which others celebrate or indeed make a condition of
the appreciation of any art whatsoever. This ought to make as clear as anything
could the ongoing dependence of postmodernism on the Western tradition: the
continued fantasy of the self as sovereign mind or textual object remaking the
world or bringing a world forward. In much postmodern art there is a mixture
of text and picture or a use of the picture as text, and so on. The Philadelphia

painters appeal to postmodern sensibilities, in part because they seem to display or embody precisely this form of textual encoding. But in fact they invert it, or it is pre-inverted in their works, answered before it was even put forward. They insist on the integrity of the pictorial as a distinctive mode of representation, or they try to subordinate the textual to the pictorial mode. They compromise the order of the word, play with it, transgress it even as they trangress aesthetic spectatorial space and maybe the law, which is itself a text.

Peto and Harnett try to collapse linguistic smeared time into the simultaneity of the pictorial order, just as Haberle tried to collapse the grand sweep of the heroic American landscape into the little still-life joke. They give you the whole book at once, give you the sheer objecthood of the book, as in a theme treated by both Harnett and Peto, *Job Lot Cheap*, in which there is a heap of presumably worthless books for sale on a shelf. They give you the look of the book without its contents, take its mysterious interior, which can be mastered only by a long study, and push it all into the colors of its covers. There is a narrative inside, but it is not present; the narrative is denarrativized, imploded into pictorial simultaneity. This is similar to the nature of poetry: to take words as objects, visible but above all audible objects, and emphasize the concreteness of the occasion of enunciation. That is what rhyme and alliteration and metre and assonance do. But Harnett and Peto and Haberle and Cope make the text into a picture and then bring the picture to presence in the illusionistic blow or gunshot. They trivialize text, play with text, reduce the anxiety of inscription and flout the laws against counterfeiting.

Now as I say, Peto's paintings in particular (or rather, uniquely for this style) approach pure abstraction. *Letter Rack on Black Door*, again, has a Mondrian-like quality. He achieved the same effect in one of the loveliest table top still lifes ever painted, *Peppermint Candy* of 1878, which depicts candy spilling out of a bag. However, again here there is a premature inversion of the idea of abstraction, premature because in fact there was no pure abstraction in Western painting in 1895 when *Letter Rack on Black Door* was painted. The paintings of Mondrian have an intense cleanliness with regard to earthly muck; they are spiritual expressions in their way, objects intended for transcendence. Indeed, pure abstraction to a large extent emerged from theosophy and other spiritual orientations for the purpose of overcoming or exceeding the mundane. And then there is the Clement Greenberg treatment of abstraction which was in part the program of later abstractionists: one removes or represses the representational content in order to create an object whose ontological integrity is the effect of its autonomy. It does not *depend*, is not a reflection of or an image of anything outside itself; it stands alone, is the object of itself, is itself an object.

One thus overcomes, at a very late date, Plato's ontology, in which the image is less real than what it represents; one makes pictures that are themselves real.

But Peto's abstraction does something very different, though also related. First of all, the most abstract of Peto's canvases were executed toward the end of his life and emerged from or rather in a lifetime of devotion to the world he depicted; the abstraction is a celebration of the beauty and at the same time the triviality of the objects he painted. In fact, he condemned himself to obscurity precisely by his absolute insistence on thematic triviality: he would not paint anything "important." He achieves an abstract effect through devotion to concreteness that is only intensified at the end of his life when he abandons any serious illusionism whatever. The flat Mondrian emerges from the flat letter rack; the point is the form of the world—which can be found in the trivial as well as in the significant, indeed is found most pointedly precisely in the trivial—not an autonomous world of form. I do believe that Peto's work is transcendent, that it is a spiritual or religious exercise. But Peto's religion is just the opposite of Madam Blavatsky's or whatever: it is a religion of the world, a pantheism that finds God in shards or fragments, which is where Emerson insisted that God should be sought. That is precisely why pantheism is a relief; it is a relief from the search for the Significant, for Mind, and so on, and a relaxation into a celebration of triviality. It is a relief from the judgment that sorts things by significance, that says: understanding is the highest and most godlike. It shows that God is as present in the shards and fragments as in the huge landscape or the important historical event. Understanding for Peto is no more godlike than a torn advertisement and is impossible without stuff like that. He gives you the traces and the preconditions of understanding but never tries to display it or celebrate it; he shows understanding in its use and in its disintegration, not in its mastery, shows you a lived-in, well-worn world and calls to you with love. And this spirituality connects Peto's work to Thoreau's, for example. If Thoreau is an "American transcendentalist" (a phrase which I have always found incredibly inept), he is a transcendentalist whose practice is an utter immanence. And that is Peto's "transcendentalism" as well: not escape or overcoming of the world but utter devotion to the world—to the lowest as the highest. This inversion of values should be experienced as a release and relief from significance. The abstraction emerges directly in the practice of immersion in the concrete, and its effect is to return us to the concrete again, now ready to immerse ourselves in it as an exercise in transcendence.

And where the Greenbergian abstractionist (Kenneth Noland or Ellsworth Kelly, say) wants to add new and better, purer, objects to the world, Peto's practice is a process of subtraction in which the abstract form never loses its status as an image or reflection, in which it is continually trying to collapse back into its object. The point of Harnett and Peto is precisely not to add objects to the world (though of course, speaking literally, they do so), but to show us the objects that are already in the world. This could not be clearer than in Haberle's *Torn in Transit* series or in the various paintings by Peto ("self-portraits") in which he pins his own previous still lifes to the wall and shows their fraying, curling edges—their status as flat objects. Here we try to *remove* works of art from the art-world, only to place them again in the world as themselves, or as objects rather than as representations. If Haberle paints a pseudo-Cole and then collapses it into a still-life element, it must constantly be borne in mind that the Haberle was itself not intended to enter the artworld, that it was destined for the barroom or store window. Even now, when I asked to see a Harnett at the Philadelphia Museum, I was conducted to the library where it was hanging unlabelled between shelves.

The "reflection of reality" that is practiced by these painters should be seen as a process of ontological simplification, and this is most obvious precisely where Peto moves toward pure abstraction. Everything is collapsed onto a plane of perfect immanence that is an intensification of pure concrete objecthood. The abstraction comes in the breakdown of an aesthetic distance that pulls you into reality, whereas the modernist abstraction is designed to impose or lengthen this distance and make you aware of its presence and your own presence in "the artworld." But as the illusionistic effect and later the play with the illusionistic effect draws you quite literally into proximity with the painting (I always get right up to the painted surface if possible, crane my neck around, check whether anyone's looking, then touch; that would be an absurd procedure to follow with an Ellsworth Kelly). You see these paintings so intensely that you encounter the pure form of the world they depict: but it is always the form *of that world*, never an addition or idealization or overcoming of the world.

In short, American precisionist still life of the late nineteenth and early twentieth centuries is an exploration of all the ways that our lives and our loves and our pleasures evade, exceed, attack, and destroy teleology and therefore history.

First, there is a celebration of and immersion in the quotidian for its own sake. This is particularly true of Harnett's work; he achieves an absolute refusal of all the grand themes and grand narratives, and this is especially pronounced because Harnett had the kind of skill in composition and rendering that could have been applied to any theme he chose with great success. Instead he chooses an immersion in the mundane that at once speaks to the craft process and focuses us into a moment—not a perfect moment, not usually an exemplary moment, not a moment in an ongoing story or project, but just a moment. He brings us face to face with the purity of pollution, the mixed life in which we are all the time engaged: the human but unprojected world of the musical instrument in silence, the unread book, the expended match. *The Faithful Colt*: just the gun on the cracked green wall, isolated from its story spatially and temporally, brought into focus by deep concentration and celebrated for being precisely what it is, precisely where it is. Harnett brings us back out of the narrative projection to the absolutely precise moment; he stills moments for us so that we can see what it would be like if the moment abided. Harnett's routine—the stuff which falls below the consciousness of most of us most of the time—learned completely, experienced deeply, is remade into art. That is, for my money, an art of truth. If you experience such painting as trivial, I agree with you and I correct you: it is profound. Its life is our life; we can take up or find our life within it. This painting is a return to where we already are.

In Peto, the routine is experienced up to the point of exhaustion, damage, despair, and death—the wear that each of us experiences as a still-life object, as a physical body in the world. The quotidian followed until, like us and with us, it peters out: then, if at no other time, we let go of our narratives: we are too tired or too dead to keep on toward the goal. The moment when, climbing a Himalaya in a blizzard, you lie down in the snow and give in, give up, let go. (That happened on Everest to a guy I knew named Scott Fisher, a guy I had seen twenty years earlier take a hundred foot freefall into a snowfield, breaking more or less everything; that life and that death have become emblematic for me and for this book.) Where we are most days: harried, hurried, without any clear sense of accomplishment, fumbling around trying to figure out what, if anything, is important. The movement toward expenditure: not the ecstatic gratuitous expenditure of the sacrificial transgression, but the feeling that we ourselves are spent. The artist: giving up his Philadelphia studio, moving to the country, selling little paintings to the tourists to make ends meet, giving up the chimeras of fame and wealth and just painting the effects of use on artifacts, painting use, painting work and working paint until he can't work any more. Then stopping in illness and pain and doing what he has done in his art for his whole life: becoming an object: old, used, over.

Haberle: first of all, the transgression, the counterfeit, made as explicit as possible. Haberle was especially fond of counterfeiting the warnings against counterfeiting. He liked girlie pictures and reproduced them in his art, an absolutely unprecedented act in art history up to that point, as far as I can see. There's even the occasional pornographic image, as in the trompe-l'oeil smorgasbord *A Bachelor's Drawer* at the Met. This work traces the life of a bachelor from various popular entertainments and solitary sexual practices through marriage and up to a booklet titled *How to Name the Baby*. It completely conflates the worlds of fine art, craft, and popular entertainment, and it does it in the most explicit way possible: each of the boundaries is delightedly transgressed. And, I might add, this is not the transgression of the ecstatic sacrifice and so on, but a transgression that is a continuous play. Haberle is as playful as any artist who ever lived, as playful as Lichtenstein. Every picture is an elaborate game filled to the brim with trickery. It's a display of wit and enjoyment that proceeds by tweaking the conventional categories and conventional tastes. The illusionary moment brings the narrative up short, and the sheer play compromises the pretensions of any serious telelogy, including those of art, but also including those of life. The bachelor on his journey into marriage is good-naturedly ridiculed, and in fact Haberle had recently married when the picture was painted, so he pokes fun at his own directionality, punctures his own pretensions.

Finally, in Chalfant, the style reaches a kind of apotheosis, if the point is, as I have held it to be, crystallinity. Here what seizes you into immediacy and immanence is above all beauty: perfect repose in the moment, a subtraction or minimalism that always maintains the most direct contact with the real object. For the experience of beauty is also, as much Western aesthetics has been devoted to showing, a return to immediacy, a point in which telelogy lets go its hold and the moment is experienced with intensity. But Chalfant's work achieves this moment in a devotion to the quotidian. He purifies what he depicts; he cuts to the chase. But he also removes all distractions from the experience of devotion to the object. As I looked at *The Old Violin* at the Delaware Art Museum, I was wondering whether it depicted a peeling white wall or rather simply had a particularly extreme case of craquelure. Then I read the card: Chalfant used a quick-drying shellac that caused the painting of the wall to crack, in order to imitate the effect of peeling paint. Here, the reflection of reality and the reality itself are collapsed perfectly: peeling paint "depicts" peeling paint: the effect is perfectly poised between the order of representation and the order of reality, between aesthetic distance and utter immersion. And in this poise, the crystalline moment emerges in ontological integrity. The real is enacted and depicted in a single gorgeous synchronic sacrament.

Of course Harnetts and Petos are still representations; according to the going theories which are certainly not entirely wrong, they still need to be read. But representation is also not where we live most of our lives; if the epistemic disaster of empiricism didn't teach us anything else, it should have taught us that. The empiricists liked pictures, mental images, ideas. They got so stuck in images that they weren't sure they could reach the world. Finally, they stopped caring whether they were stuck or not and said it really made no difference. The people I have been attacking in this book like words and think pictures are passe or think pictures are words. But the same disaster looms as loomed for empiricists: oops, here we are behind the veil of words. Of course these various veils are comforting; they help us attenuate our experience in imagination, which is really why we became scholars and retreated to the library in the first place: we were trying to avoid people. I try to avoid people too, but now I want to say something in their favor. One good thing about people: they're not words. It is a measure of just how bizarre things have gotten that that last sentence expresses a radical or maybe reactionary sentiment.

It is not wrong to say that touching someone is a form of communication. And it is not wrong to say that touching people often or even always makes use of various quasi-linguistic conventions; different sorts of touch *mean* different things in the vernaculars of physical contact between human bodies. Once, Mali and I kissed about death. But if you think that touching is entirely a linguistic or quasi-linguistic symbol system, then I think you have probably never really touched or been touched by anybody, or that you are now looking for a way out of dealing with that experience. Even Harnetts and Petos leave us a little dignity, especially since they've entered the museum system: we can gaze, decode, appreciate. But to revel in someone else's body or to kick someone else's ass, or to do both serially or simultaneously is not by and large a very dignified procedure: it's time to wallow in mammality. Time, eventually, for the chatterbox in your head to shut up so you can just get into it. There's no decent sex that doesn't turn off the chatter; no decent fight that doesn't reach the point of intensity at which you're just flailing and scratching and clawing, at which you've quit talking to yourself. Finally, all that noise—the grunt, the moan, the rasp of pain or pleasure—is a way back toward the silence from which we emerged.

II

Here is how Thoreau begins his great essay "Walking":

> I wish to speak a word for Nature, for absolute freedom and wildness, as contrasted with a freedom and a culture merely civil,—to regard man as an inhabitant, or a part and parcel of Nature, rather than a member of society. I wish to make an extreme statement, if

so I may make an emphatic one, for there are enough champions of
civilization: the minister, and the school-committee, and every one
of you will take care of that.[2]

Yes, every one of us will take care of that. We all speak, insofar as we speak, as
champions of the human; people taught us to speak, and they teach us still, for
to speak is to speak out of a shifting human crowd into a shifting human crowd.
To speak against the human, or in favor of the inhuman, to speak wildly on
behalf of wildness, is already to be embroiled in hypocrisy. To speak is to be
engulfed in the human, swept away into the chattering of millions for millen-
nia. Even our silences and solitudes are humanized; even our inmost recesses
have been reached by the chatter. We learned by logging and paving the world
to log and pave ourselves, until we seem to be perfectly processed, until even
our killings are human.

I doubt that Thoreau could have imagined our saturation by the human;
I doubt that he could have tolerated our soddenness. There are whole philosophical edifices today in which there is no mention at all of anything that is
not a human being or an object made by a human being: Wittgenstein's, Foucault's. There are environments so humanized that it is a pain and an entrapment to be a human being in them; in the concrete and broken glass and broken persons, we are so human that we're dying, because we've already killed
everything else. There are human environments engineered at such a scale that
they dwarf the human body, reduce the human to a pure and puny humanity.
There are environments so perfectly processed that animal bodies like ours
seem disconcerting and unclean in them: gleaming corporate interiors where
it is impertinent to be a mammal. There are environments where form follows
function so closely that, God help us, there is nothing that is not comprehensible or that stands in excess to the human. There are environments so perfectly
and so frozenly humanized that it is impossible to be human in them. There are
environments where there are no trees, and environments where the trees are
tended as decorations, as ornaments or badges of status. There are environments
in which trees must be caged for their own survival, wherein people must be
constrained from tearing them out by the roots.

Like Thoreau, I'd like to say a few words about getting less human, a few
words that are self-immolating, words that attack themselves for being words,
that attack me for writing them, attack you for reading them. I'd like to explore

2. Henry David Thoreau, "Walking," reprinted in *Civil Disobedience and Other Essays*
(New York: Dover, 1993), p. 49.

whether it is possible to stop being artifacts, or to realize the ways in which we still exceed artifactuality; whether there is a power in us that is not given to us or taken from other human beings, whether we can make ourselves wilder, destroy ourselves as we are, or love ourselves as we are, find again a context in which "the social" takes place—a world to which we are open or which opens us to itself. "Life consists with wildness. The most alive is the wildest. Not yet subdued to man, its presence refreshes him" ("Walking," 62). "There is in my nature, methinks, a singular yearning toward wildness. I know of no redeeming qualities in myself but a sincere love for some things."[3] We need what we cannot hold or encompass, what demands no recompense and is pitiless and deaf to pity; we need what collapses us into pain and ecstasy, need what we can never know. The cry of the newborn or of the dying is an inhuman cry, primal in its fury or its despair or its suffering or its perfect freedom or its perfect fatedness, an invasion of the human world by the human body. "There may be an excess of cultivation as well as of anything else, until civilization becomes pathetic. A highly cultivated man,—all whose bones can be bent! whose heaven-born virtues are but good manners! . . . We would not always be soothing and taming nature, breaking the horse and the ox, but sometimes ride the horse wild and chase the buffalo" (A Week, 46). "In proportion as our inward life fails, we go more constantly and desperately to the post-office. You may depend on it, that the poor fellow who walks away with the greatest number of letters, proud of his extensive correspondence, has not heard from himself this long while."[4]

I have struggled for a long time with the following question: what is the place of human beings in nature? And I have always answered in roughly the same terms: human beings are "part and parcel" of nature, are as natural as boulders. There "ought" to be no distinction between the natural and the artificial; there "ought" to be no distinction between what human beings make and what we find or what finds us. "Civilization does but dress men. . . . Inside the civilized man stands the savage still in the place of honor" (A Week, 281). Why, then, do we (HDT and I) flee the human, hate it, fear it? Why does it arouse our loathing, our claustrophobia? What are we fleeing? Ourselves? What are we fleeing? The people we love? If you haven't seen that Thoreau hates and fears the human, you need to read again; he is a solitary. "I find it wholesome to be alone the greater part of the time. To be in company, even with the best, is soon

---

3. *A Week on the Concord and Merrimack Rivers*, reprinted in *Henry David Thoreau* (Library of America, 1985), p. 45. Further page references are to this volume unless otherwise noted.

4. "Life Without Principles," in *Civil Disobedience and Other Essays*, p. 84.

wearisome and dissipating. I love to be alone. I never found the companion that was so companionable as solitude. We are for the most part more lonely when we go abroad among men than when we stay in our chambers" (*Walden*, 430). Thoreau is the Garbo of the natural: a recluse, a man who criticized architecture and found the greatest sublimity where there were no people. Every walk he took was a walk away from human beings and human things. Famously: "If you are ready to leave father and mother, and brother and sister, and wife and child and friends, and never see them again,—if you have paid your debts, and made your will, and settled all your affairs, and are a free man, then you are ready for a walk" ("Walking," 50). Thoreau appears to associate all human relations with unfreedom; he thinks to be free is to be alone.

"Nowadays almost all man's improvements, so called, as the building of houses, and the cutting down of the forest and of all large trees, simply deform the landscape, and make it more and more tame and cheap" ("Walking," 53). Why is a forest beautiful and a parking lot ugly? Why does the one draw us out of ourselves and into God, the other push us into ourselves and away? Not, I guess, in virtue of the fact that the forest is natural and the parking lot artificial. Not, I guess, because the parking lot is created out of destruction; all things are created out of destruction. What do we want when we want wildness, HDT and I? What would we do with it if we had it? If we had it, would we still want it? Could there be a power in wildness that is lost when wildness is tamed? What could it mean to tame wildness, in a world in which people are animals? What is happening when we break what is wild, subdue it—is it wildness breaking wildness wildly? Why does what we break in this way seem to so flat? Why do the animals we breed seem so predictable or stupid? "I rejoice that horses and steers have to be broken before they can be made the slaves of men, and that men themselves have some wild oats left to sow before they become submissive members of society" ("Walking," 67).

Wildness is dangerous. To live wildly or to live in the wilderness is to live a short life and a painful life. Perhaps, then, to tame something means to make it safe, safe for us. Why then, what is wrong with safety? For God's sake, it beats continual endangerment. And yet what we have made safe, humanized, first, bores us. And second, it endangers us too, for there are wild animals in it, even if none but persons, the most dangerous predators of persons. Why is it that we can always humanize trees and animals and mountains and deserts but not always people? Why do we exceed our own grasp?

And, in a situation in which human beings are natural things, what are human beings doing yearning toward nature? What would it mean to be reconciled to that of which we are all along part and parcel? In what sense have we become distanced from nature, and isn't the possibility of that precisely what I am denying? What do we yearn toward when we yearn toward nature? Does it make sense to yearn toward what is already obviously the case? How have we gotten into the bizarre Kierkegaardian position of wanting what we already have, of wanting to be what we already are? And what would it be like to come to possess what we never lost, or to become what we never ceased to be?

Alright, that's too many questions, isn't it?

I've calmed a bit now. I wrote that last bit in Manhattan. I felt enclosed in the little apartment where I stayed with a lover and argued about "social constructionism." I felt almost as enclosed when I got outside, and the crowds milled and the buildings lowered. As I say, I think Thoreau was a claustrophobe, that he kept feeling enclosed by people and their things, that he kept wanting out. The quotation that opens this discussion of Thoreau expresses a disdain, found throughout Thoreau's writings, for human institutions and their "representatives," or more accurately for the way people get reduced to or enclosed in representations by and in institutions, by and in themselves. (That particular claustrophobia connects Thoreau and Foucault, by the way.) To tame something is to reduce it to a function, to simplify it toward usefulness, to rub off the raw and inconvenient and living edges. "I love man-kind, but I hate the institutions of dead un-kind" (*A Week*, 106). "Wherever a man goes, men will pursue and paw him with their dirty institutions" (*Walden*, 459). "In short, as a snow-drift is formed where there is a lull in the wind, so, one would say, where there is a lull in the truth, an institution springs up. But the truth blows right over it, nonetheless, and at length blows it down" ("Life Without Principle," 89). Maybe that's why what is tamed is dull in our eyes: it surprises us less because it does what we want. We want what *doesn't* do what we want. That's what "refreshes" us. The minister and school committee are tame in this sense like hens: the perfect school committee would not consist of organisms at all but of sheer functions.

So anyway, I took a walk out of the Village looking for an open space where I could breathe. I finally dodged through the traffic on the West Side Highway and walked out onto a pier on the Hudson. It was made of concrete. There were a lot of people on it. And there were chain-link and barbed-wire fences and highway-type barricades. But people had cut up the fences so that they could get out near the water. There seemed to be a gay side and a straight side; both sides were drinking and drugging sides, and brown bags were making the rounds. The people lying out on the gay side were sunbathing; anyone lying out on the straight side had passed out. I gingerly picked my way through the bodies, hoping to avoid—for a few moments, anyway—solicitations of money or sex. And I looked at the river: there was nothing to occlude my sight until my eye met the Jersey shore. I breathed more fully than I had in a couple of days, all the while keeping one eye cocked for who was approaching. I started wondering if that water down there could give me all I needed of the nonhuman; I was contemplating a move to New York, wondering what it would be like to live there.

A few days later I drove home on the Jersey Turnpike. I live out in rural Maryland, in the cornfields. The first thing I did when I got home was walk out to some woods behind my house. It was a perfectly fresh spring day (May 14, to be precise), full of the scent and vibration that plants emanate when they're starting to grow. I sat by a creek and prayed. I watched the water, alternating my attention between the braiding patterns and smooth pools (the texture of the flow), the minnows suspended in that medium (and themselves of the nature of water), the stones and mud in the creek bed, the moving reflection of the trees. The sound of water flowing through rock brought me peace. "He who hears the rippling of rivers in these degenerate days will not utterly despair" (*A Week*, 272). Admittedly, that peace only lasted for a few moments. I'm not good at peace.

Now it's a few days after that, and I'm lonely. My lover in New York is a voice over a wire or a text e-mailed. My kids aren't around. I've got no friends around here (I'm not good at that, either). Maybe, I'm thinking, Thoreau wasn't such an isolate after all ("we cannot have too many friends" *A Week*, 224). So I kind of wish I was back in New York, where there's a restaurant or a bar every few yards, where everybody is so weird that no one notices that I am, too, where there's more than one person. Like Thoreau, I feel lonely with and drained by people, but unlike Thoreau, I'm morbid and obsessive rather than "wholesome" when I'm alone too long. I turn on the television; the human voices comfort me. I turn on the stereo; I want to listen to something very human, like Annie Lennox or Shirley Caesar. But it doesn't work all that well, and before long I feel absolutely trapped in the confines of my own head, in the language I speak to myself. The longer I'm by myself, the worse it gets.

You see the dilemma: can't live with 'em, and though you can shoot 'em, maybe that's not such a hot idea. Besides, there are a lot of them. (If you're wondering, I wasn't all that ecstatic in the suburbs, either.) And I definitely can't live without them. I *need* people, need them badly, perhaps worst when I'm working desperately on how to get rid of them. And I love people, too. They're cuddly.

So then we run into the parallel set of questions. We're embedded in the social. The cornfields are as human an environment as Greenwich Village. We can't escape the social: it made us, is making us, has given us to speak: for it, against it, or about something else. When I am alone, I am still surrounded, connected by memory and projection and by an elaborate web of wires with people all over. I am not alone when I am alone: I carry within me my parents, my dead brothers and my live one, my lovers, my teachers, anyone who has looked on me with affection or contempt or amused or unamused indifference. I have been shaped by them, by our human rituals and practices, like a piece of jade carved and polished, as Confucius, that champion of the social, put it. So what does it mean to yearn toward people, to feel alone? In a world where there is no surcease from our permeation by the human, why is there a zone of indifference, disconnection? Why, when I am looked at by someone, can I usually tell that they do not see me? "It is rare that one gets seriously looked at" (*A Week*, 52). What would it mean to get connected to the social networks and social practices in which one is all the time embedded? How could I ever be alone? Why do I usually *feel* alone when aloneness is an impossible fantasy or nightmare? What would it mean to affirm that I am socially constructed when that affirmation is socially constructed, when there seems to be no "outside" from which to see the social?

What I'd really like to do is leave all those questions sitting there as questions; there's a certain wildness to them as questions; to answer them is to tame them. But I guess I'm not able, finally, to do that. So here's my dilemma. I hold that people are as natural as wolves or buffalo. I can deploy no distinction between the natural and the artificial. But in fact I *use* that distinction all the time. I think of the traces of the human in the woods as pollution. I'm more at peace in "unspoiled" nature than anywhere else, except perhaps in the bedroom of my lover (often I'm not at peace there, either). I think the distinction is incomprehensible, indefensible. But the distinction is decidedly active in my life, determining such decisions as where I will live and where I will travel. Obviously, my own internal conflicts do not bear on the legitimacy of the distinction per se, but I'm not that interested, any more, in the legitimacy of distinctions per se; I'm trying to figure out how the hell to live without hypocrisy.

Well, then, let's try this: the natural/artificial distinction, which amounts, finally, to no less than the claim that human beings are separated by an insuperable gap from the order and disorder of nature, that is, from the world, is indeed a complete mess. It is a delusion. We are fused with the natural environment, are without remainder of the earth. But delusions have concrete effects; in this case, they have effects made of concrete. How we think of ourselves in relation to the earth actually effects ways of being on the earth. The Western tradition conceives of a separation, conceives of the earth as inanimate and unintelligent, and of ourselves as animate and intelligent. It conceives of the earth as means, persons as ends. It conceives of human action technologically, or according to the canons of practical rationality. We want to *liquidate* means into ends; to regard something as a mere means is to want to *annihilate* it into our end, as I have discussed elaborately. The means are always simultaneously what enables us toward the end and what constitutes the barrier to the end; it is the recalcitrance of means, their opacity, their intrinsic character, that delineates them as something to be overcome even as, in their character as means, they are what enables us to overcome them. Now we are in precisely that relation to the wild earth. It is what we use for our purposes, and it is what frustrates the immediate realization of our purposes. The stubborn physical thereness of the wild earth, when it is regarded as a means, is a continual barrier, whereas we experience our own purposes and our own linguistic representations as liquid and transparent; their transportation to "mental reality," the feeling we have that they are already ours, that they are "human" purposes and representations, gives us a great feeling of comfort or of ease, even as it increases our frustration with what exceeds the human.

Again, that's a delusion: we are also recalcitrant to the operations of our own will. And our representative and linguistic capacities are received from the earth, are not, finally, human. But this structure of being, this way of life, sets the human against what is wild. First, it seeks to tame or humanize the self, to reduce it to agency. Second, it seeks to humanize other human beings, to make them useful, to reduce them to functions and institutions. Third, it seeks to humanize nature, to break its wildness toward comprehensibility, to make it functional. "Practical rationality" is about one thing: domination. It plays for domination in every possible arena: in the self, in the social, in the more-than-social. And it plays for domination through the structures of consciousness: through the formulation of ends and the administration in imagination of means, it requires language and reduces consciousness to language. Hence "detachment": the structure of representation in the West is a structure of detachment. And hence, out of delusion, annihilation: we seek to flatten, destroy, process toward perfect utility, as Dewey says and recommends. So we begin to experience ourselves as things that dominate and destroy the earth, begin to experience ourselves as distanced, dominating, and, finally, as destructive. What we think of as our destruction is perfectly real: we pave over, we spew toxins, we replace what's there with what we put there. But it cannot, finally, be a matter of the supernatural destroying the natural, of consciousness destroying the inanimate, because consciousness is an animal function and the earth is animate. If there is a "solution," it does not lie in establishing a connection of the human and the natural; that was never broken. It does not lie in preserving resources; that's just a more circumspect version of the same old shit. The solution is ripping apart practical rationality and its temporal/linguistic order, showing it to be delusory, finding a new and more real way to be.

Now that, I propose, is something that wilderness can teach us. To walk into a serious wilderness (which is admittedly a whole lot more difficult than it was in 1850) is be overwhelmed by what stands in excess to our purposes; it is to enter a place where human purpose is puny. In the wilderness we experience the powerlessness not only of ourselves (an experience which can be had all day every day anywhere: try dealing with the IRS or the Transit Authority; try dealing with your own desires), but the powerlessness of the human quite in general. Wilderness stands so obviously in excess to human purpose, is so obviously indifferent to human purposes, that perhaps we can get a little more indifferent to our own purposes there, stop struggling to reduce everything to means which we can annihilate into ends.

> It is difficult to conceive of a region uninhabited by man. We habitually presume his presence and influence everywhere. And yet we have not seen pure Nature, unless we have seen her thus vast and drear and inhuman, though in the midst of cities. Nature was here [in the forests of Maine] something savage and awful, though beautiful. I looked with awe at the ground I trod on, to see what the Powers had made there, the form and fashion and material of their work. This was that Earth of which we have heard, made out of Chaos and Old Night. Here was no man's garden, but the unhandselled globe. It was not lawn, nor pasture, nor mead, nor woodland, nor lea, nor arable, nor waste-land. It was the fresh and natural surface of the planet Earth, as it was made for ever and ever,—to be the dwelling of man, we say,—so Nature made it, and man may use it if he can. Man was not to be associated with it. It was matter, vast, terrific,—not his Mother Earth that we have heard of, not for him to tread on or be buried in,—no, it were being too familiar even to let his bones lie there,—the home, this, of Necessity and fate. There was there felt the presence of a force not bound to be kind to man. It was a place of heathenism and superstitious rites,—to be inhabited by men nearer of kin to the rocks and to wild animals than we. . . . What is it to be admitted to a museum, to see a myriad of particular things, compared with being shown some star's surface, some hard matter in its home! I stand in awe of my body, this matter to which I am bound has become so strange to me. I fear not spirits, ghosts, of which I am one,—*that* my body might,— but I fear bodies, I tremble to meet them. What is this Titan that has possession of me? Talk of mysteries!—Think of our life in nature,—daily to be shown matter, to come into contact with

it,—rocks, trees, wind on our cheeks! the *solid* earth! the *actual*
world! the *common sense! Contact! Contact! Who are we? where* are
we? (*The Maine Woods*, 645–46)

That is an amazing passage. It says, first, that to experience wilderness is to
experience the world as indifferent to our ends, as not made for our sakes and
not transformable by will, or rather, only transformable by an incredibly long,
elaborate process, and then only to a limited extent. We may use it if we can,
but it was not made for us. To experience wilderness is to be *dwarfed* and it is
to be dwarfed in a particular way: by fate.

For if there is one thing that we can pit against practical rationality, it is
fate, and traditions that emphasize fatality are always opposed to the annihilation of the world into means, always hold that to be an illusion. To experience
fatality is to experience the dissolution of the delusion of agency, hence of the
delusion of human detachment from nature. *You can reconcile yourself to fate, or to
what is fated, or what comes to you as a fate, but you cannot use it.* That makes you
wild, kin to rocks, because to be tame is precisely to enter into the "freedom"
of agency and the reduction toward use. (It is "freedom of the will" that sepa-
rates us inexorably in delusion from nature.)

The perfect contrast here would be of the natural history museum to
the Maine woods, the structure of taxonomic representation and purification
and humanization to the bewildering or overwhelming surface of a star. The
former displays the organization of things simultaneously for appreciation
and for possible use, assures us of our power and of the victory of the human.
It demystifies, educates. The latter overwhelms our categories and resists our
uses, bewilders us into a realization of our vast and beautiful ignorance,
assures us that somewhere there is a surcease from our own power, shows us
our own wildness. And hence it brings us face to face with our own complete actuality and physicality, lets us experience ourselves again as bodies.
That means that it brings us into identity with it, collapses the delusion of
distance imposed by the structure of language and representation as it breaks
our wills, teaches us the mysteries of our bodies, teaches us our unfreedom,
reconciles us with the world, with fate. *That* is why we need wilderness: not
because it is more natural than Manhattan, but because it teaches us animal-
ity and fatality, lets us experience Manhattan too as wild. "I have been into
the lumber-yard, and the carpenter's shop, and the tannery, and the lamp-
black-factory, and the turpentine clearing; but when at length I saw the tops
of the pines waving and reflecting the light at a distance high over all the
rest of the forest, I realized that the former were not the highest use of the
pine. It is not their bones or hide or tallow that I love most. It is the living

spirit of the tree, not its spirit of turpentine, with which I sympathize, and which heals my cuts" (*The Maine Woods*, 685).

In the West, the tradition that most emphasizes fate is Stoicism. And in fact Thoreau was in many ways a Stoic. Stoicism is, I think, the great Greek alternative to Aristotle. Though there is an obvious influence of Aristotle on at least the later Stoics, there is a resistance to and a rejection of the most basic elements of Aristotelian accounts of human action and of cosmology. The fundamental tenet of Stoic ethics and cosmology is a relinquishment of the pretension to power over the world and a corresponding account of that world as indifferent to human purposes. And Stoicism's basic account of time is not linear but cyclical; the Stoics deployed a doctrine of time that is very close to Nietzsche's eternal recurrence. There is no gainsaying the cycle of time, no controlling it; every event occurs exactly as it must. Cleanthes's prayer expresses fate as follows:

> Lead me, O Zeus, and lead me thou, O fate,
> Unto that place where you have stationed me:
> I shall not flinch, but follow: and if become
> Wicked I should refuse, still, I must follow.[5]

This expresses the view that resistance to fate, free will (at least as it concerns external actions in the world) is a delusion, and that delusion is wickedness; it would make Aristotelian practical rationality ridiculous. I can resist my fate in imagination, but resisting it in actuality is utterly hopeless; as Spinoza said, freedom in the traditional sense is a delusion based on ignorance. I will follow; I must follow. And peace will come in an allowance of myself to follow, an allowance of myself to be in the world of nature.

Now the Greek word *physis*—nature—is a much-vexed term, particularly as it is used by the Stoics. Just as does the English word, it can mean the entire physical system of the universe (and the Stoics regarded the human soul, and God, as material—they were monists) and also the being of human beings: "human nature." Sandbach among others has termed the word "ambiguous" for that reason. But in fact, as in Thoreau, the word is univocal because we're in a cosmology in which the being of human beings is connected to the being of the universe in all ways simultaneously, in which human *physis* is an expression of and a microcosm of universal *physis*. We are located not in human time but

---

5. Quoted in F. H. Sandbach, *The Stoics* (Indianapolis: Hackett, 1989), p. 37. I have altered the translation slightly.

in the time of nature; our nature *is* nature. And if there is an overwhelming emphasis on "reason" (*logos*, language) in the Stoics, and a distinction between human beings and animals and inanimate objects made on the basis of the fact that human beings have *logos* (perhaps the most characteristic assertion of Greek philosophy, perhaps the founding thought of the Western tradition), it must also be borne in mind that the Stoic conception of *logos* is not primarily that of Plato or Aristotle, but of Heraclitus. And for Heraclitus, *logos* is fire, flux; it is an aspect of a changing universe in its cyclical time, not a humanistic practical faculty, or an abstractive faculty yielding access to a higher plane of being. "The cosmos, the same for all, none of the gods nor humans has made, but it was always and is and shall be: an ever-living fire being kindled in measures and being extinguished in measures."[6] So I would like to read the centrality of *logos* to the Stoics as an assertion of a distinctive place for human beings in a universal flux. This place is not the ability to control that flux or even primarily to understand it in an Aristotelian taxonomy, but an expression of the faculty that allows us consciously to reconcile ourselves to it. What is distinctive about the human, then, is that this reconciliation is possible for us, as it is not for other animals. Because of the delusion of our power over time, this reconciliation is an *achievement:*

> Mindful, therefore, of this ordaining we should go to receive instruction, not in order to change the constitution of things,—for this is neither vouchsafed us nor is it better that it should be,—but in order that, things about us being as they are and as their nature is, we may, for our own part, keep our wills in harmony with what happens. For, look you, can we escape from men? And how is it possible? But can we, if they associate with us, change them? And who vouchsafes us that power?[7]

This is a paradoxical agency: try to do whatever happens. Or else it is the annihilation of agency into presence; the reconciliation is to a non-narrative order. And it is in bringing us forward into the achievement of reconciliation that Stoic ethics recognizes its distinctive task. "I must die," says Epictetus, "Must I, then, die whining too? I must be fettered: and wailing too?" (*Discourses*, 13). And, quoting Chrysippus: "If I really knew that it was ordained for me to be ill at this present moment, I would even seek illness" (*Discourses*, 249). And what

---

6. Heraclitus, fragment 22B30, trans. Richard D. McKirahan in *A Presocratics Reader*, Patricia Curd, ed. (Indianapolis: Hackett, 1996), p. 37.

7. Epictetus, *The Discourses*, W. A. Oldfather, trans. (Cambridge Mass.: Harvard University Press (Loeb Classical Library), 19250, p. 93.

the whole quotation says is that if I understood myself as fully a part of the universe, I could reconcile myself to my part in the universe.

"How [will I die]? As becomes a man who is giving back what is another's" (*Discourses*, 15). Our lives and our bodies, for Epictetus, do not belong to ourselves, a beautiful conception which certainly precludes an Aristotelian conception of agency; agency is essentially the possession of our bodies by ourselves. The characteristic mistake or idiosyncracy of Stoicism, however, as Pascal recognized, is that it holds our own thoughts and desires to be within our control, a vestige of Platonic dualism in the Stoic's monistic cosmos. But death for Epictetus is a return that expresses our identity with the cosmic order: "the dewdrop sinks into the shining sea." Death encapsulates both our fatedness and our identity with *physis*, the universal flux in which we participate, the *logos* in ourselves in identity with the *logos* of all that is, the order that is made in constant derangement.

Physis, for Thoreau—our own and the world's—is expressed in wildness and is associated by Thoreau with *life*; that's why it's a perfect pole to institution. Our power is a killing. Our separation from the disorder of nature in imagination is an imagination of death, because we have our life in our bodies and because we are bodies on the living earth. When we "control" something, that usually means, in practical terms, that we reduce the life within it, or appropriate its life to ourselves. "Whatever part the whip has touched is thenceforth palsied" ("Walking," 67). When we "control" ourselves we distance ourselves from ourselves, purport to become wills instead of bodies, reduce the life within us: that is the disease that Stoicism set itself to treat. "Life consists with wildness. The most alive is the wildest. Not yet subdued to man, its presence refreshes him. One who pressed forward incessantly and never rested from his labors, who grew fast and made infinite demands on life, would always find himself in a new country or wilderness, and surrounded by the raw material of life. He would be climbing over the prostrate stems of forest-trees" ("Walking," 62).

As we have seen, to seize control of something or break it is to insert it into human time, the time defined by project. Thoreau is as thorough in despising the life of project as is Bataille; he despised the whole language of productivity, efficiency, and so forth then coming into vogue in American capitalism. Above all he hated what that does to our time; he wanted a work that could be done in love and in loving awareness of the present moment. My whole aesthetics could be derived from "Life Without Principle." And in "Walking," he says:

> Above all, we cannot afford not to live in the present.... Unless our philosophy hears the cock crow in every barn-yard within our horizon, it is belated. That sound commonly reminds us that we are

growing rusty and antique in our employments and habits of thought. His philosophy comes down to a more recent time than ours. There is something suggested by it that is a newer testament,— the gospel according to the present moment. ("Walking," p. 73)

In this (as in so many ways) Thoreau prefigures Nietzsche, the Nietzsche of "On the Utility and Liability of History for Life":

> [I]t is always just one thing alone that makes happiness happiness: the ability to forget, or, expressed in more scholarly fashion, the capacity to feel ahistorically over the entire course of its duration. Anyone who cannot forget the past entirely and set himself down on the threshold of the present moment, anyone who cannot stand, without dizziness or fear, on one single point like a victory goddess, will never know what happiness is; worse, he will never do anything that makes others happy....All action requires forgetting, just as the existence of all organic things requires not only light, but darkness as well....In other words, it is possible to live almost without memory, indeed, to live happily, as the animals show us; but without forgetting it is utterly impossible to live at all.[8]

What Thoreau and Nietzsche are on about here is a deadening of persons by the dead weight of the past, and concomitantly, the ahistoricity of wild nature. But Nietzsche might also have talked of the dead weight of the "historical" or projected future, of the whole impulse to *order* temporality—to put *it* under control, make *it* a technological resource—an impulse which is, as I have said, perfectly poised opposite the Stoic conception of fate. In the "historical consciousness," the present is significant as a location in a linear temporality; but then, that is a significance shared by *every* moment of the time line. In the historical consciousness, the present has no presence, no wildness, no strangeness; it is *comprehensible*. This is what relates narrative history to science: they are modes of control; science erases temporality in taxonomy, but history "coordinates," compresses, or controls temporality, makes it into a resource in practical rationality. For finally it is time itself that is brought to heel, that is broken or tamed in a technological mode of living or in a narrative of history. For Thoreau, we stand in need of a "gospel according to the present moment," or else, to repeat, there is nothing to order.

It is interesting that Nietzsche and Thoreau see happiness precisely as the annihilation of history, and this can easily enough be sucked back into a

---

8. Freidrich Nietzsche, "On the Utility and Liability of History for Life," *Unfashionable Observations*, trans. Richard T. Gray (Stanford: Stanford University Press, 1995), pp. 88–89.

technology of forgetting. But then again, many cultures have sought renewal, or even meaning, in an annihilation of history, though an annihilation that makes use of narrative. Here, history gets opposed to mythology, and linear to cyclical time; renewal is achieved by an enactment of the creation narrative.

That, I think, is a function of Nietzsche's and of the Stoics' eternal return: besides being a thought experiment in the affirmation of the world, it is an experiment in the recovery of cyclical time. For that reason, it is also a recovery of ceremonial time, which applies the squandering of resources in the present to a reconnection to cyclical temporality, to a renewal or new beginning that annihilates history. That is the appropriate function of the sacrifice or the ceremonial orgy: it demonstrates by senseless expenditure the withdrawal of a commitment to the future which is also a withdrawal from history. It makes possible an emphatic presence in which time, as it were, begins again. Mircea Eliade, with astonishing documentation to back him up, describes the essence of ceremony in many cultures as "the abolition of time through the imitation of archetypes and the repetition of paradigmatic gestures." He continues:

> A sacrifice, for example, not only exactly reproduces the initial sacrifice revealed by a god *ab origine*, at the beginning of time, it also takes place at the same primordial mythical moment; in other words, every sacrifice repeats the initial sacrifice and coincides with it. All sacrifices are performed at the same mythical instant of the beginning; through the paradox of rite, profane time and duration are suspended. . . . Insofar as an act (or an object) acquires a certain reality through the repetition of certain paradigmatic gestures, and acquires it through that alone, there is an implicit abolition of profane time, of duration, of "history."[9]

As I say, Eliade demonstrates this elaborately out of the world's spiritual traditions. But what he could have added is that the regeneration of time, the re-enactment of the primordial or creative moment, happens by means of the call to presence; the abolition of history occurs whenever there is an enactment of complete presence. "Sacrifice," writes Bataille, "is the antithesis of production."[10] Or, time begins again at every moment that is actually experienced. Eliade's definition of *history* is "the irreversibility of events." But one might equally say that history is the deferral of presence. Eliade's definition is tendentious in this

---

9. Mircea Eliade, *The Myth of the Eternal Return, Or, Cosmos and History* (Princeton: Princeton University Press, 1974), p. 35.

10. Georges Bataille, *Theory of Religion*, trans. Robert Hurley (New York: Zone, 1992), p. 49.

respect—that we all know, more or less, that time cannot be reversed—so that Eliade ends up characterizing as "primitive" or "archaic" the vain battle of persons against historical time. But if we think of the "primitive" sacrificial or dramatic attitude as a call to complete presence, as what "halts" the phenomenology of project and hence renews or re-establishes time, then we need not think of such temporalities as "primitive" or even false. Rather, we might think of each moment as a birth, as an arrival in presence. That would not be perverse or primitive, because it is true insofar as existence cannot be deferred. Or rather, maybe it's perverse, primitive, *and* true.

For such reasons, Thoreau prefers mythology to literature: "I walk out into a Nature such as the old prophets and poets, Menu [Manu], Moses, Homer, Chaucer, walked in. You may name it America, but it is not America: neither Americus Vespucius, not Columbus, nor the rest were discoverers of it. There is a truer account of it in mythology than in any history of America, so called, that I have seen" ("Walking," 54). The history of America is the history of a project. The name of America is the name of that project. But the mythology of America (and surely Thoreau means, at least in part, the mythology of the "American" "Indian") is the trace of the *presence* of America, a presence that abides. That is, it presents us, in its mythology and its wildness, with the abiding possibility of our coming to presence within it. This is what mythology is *for*, finally, as Eliade saw: coming to presence on the earth. "You will perceive that I demand something which no Augustan nor Elizabethan age, which no *culture*, in short, can give. Mythology comes nearer to it than anything" ("Walking," 65). Mythology is different from literature in at least this: that it is meant to be enacted; not as an entertainment, or merely as an entertainment, but as a coming-to-presence in ceremony, as an expression of the claim of the present to abide. A creation myth that has ceased to be enacted has become literature or a museum piece.

Yet it is worth emphasizing that the emergence of history from myth, of project from presence, proceeds by fits and starts and is never complete. As quickly as the future annihilates the present, the present annihilates or devours the future—both the point of sacrifice and the paradox of project. It is a familiar point that Western drama emerges from ritual enactments of myth, or from the Dionysian orgy in which the future is annihilated in intoxication. That is where the "canon" begins, and we have not fully emerged even yet. Thoreau looks to literature or music for its wildness or strangeness, for its capacities for renewal. "There is something in a strain of music, whether produced by an instrument or by the human voice,—take the sound of a bugle on a summer night for instance,—which by its wildness, to speak without satire, reminds me of the cries emitted by wild beasts in their native forests" ("Walking," 66). I think many of us experience music as a call to presence. And our arts, as I have argued, despite all their historicity, despite all their secularization, despite all their segregation in the life of the culture, still have their moments of wildness; even in decadence they occur in ceremonial time.

What's hopeful about our entrapment in the human, conceived as being a matter of linguistic representation and of practical rationality and of historical time, is precisely that it is a delusion. We are wilder than we think we are: even the natural history museum and the parking lot and the accountant are wild. That is easy to see when you note the physical recalcitrances of the museum or the parking lot, the opacity of the matter that composes them, the fact that we've worked *with* rather than directly against that matter if we've been able to make anything at all. Think of every aspect of the accountant that is not pure accounting: his organs, his hair, his vices, his stupidities, his loves. Perhaps we can recover a sense of what, in language, evades or compromises the social, or recapture a sense of the wildness of language, the ways it already exceeds the human and makes use of the nonhuman, is bequeathed fatality by the nonhuman. After all, language is itself a recalcitrant medium. Maybe we are suspended in it like fish in water, but sometimes the water is muddy, sometimes the fish is swept away or dashed to bits or beached or all three in the flood. Even if language is human, it has all the beautiful stupidity and resistance to will that is found in the human, that is found everywhere in nature.

Many times in his writings, Thoreau compares writing to farming:

> You shall see rude and sturdy, experienced and wise men, keeping their castles, or teaming up their summer's wood, or chopping alone in the woods, men fuller of talk and rare adventure in the sun and wind and rain, than a chestnut is of meat; who were out not only in '75 and 1812, but have been out every day of their lives; greater men than Homer, or Chaucer, or Shakespeare, only they never got time to say so; they never took to the way or writing. Look at their fields, and imagine what they might write, if ever they should put pen to paper. Or what have they not written on the face of the earth already, clearing, and burning, and scratching, and harrowing, and subsoiling, in and in, and out and out, and over and over, again and again, erasing what they had already written for want of parchment. (*A Week*, 9)

Even writing, after all, makes use of the physical; it is the physical act of a physical body using physical bodies (yes, even at the computer). Farming changes the landscape, "humanizes" it, but farming is a continual mutual physical adjustment of land and man; farming is, or may be, a *devotion* to land. It brings forth things for us out of the land and transforms the land into something that brings forth things for us. But it works in and with fatality; farming that does not acknowledge the seasons, the drought, the deluge, the character of the soil, is not even farming. What compromises practical rationality is not a letting-go of ends, but a devotion to means, a love of the land and of the process of altering it and being weathered in one's alteration of it. But then, if we thought of farming as a kind of writing, or writing as a kind of farming, what would we be thinking?

> The weapons with which we have gained our most important victories, which should be handed down as heirlooms from father to son, are not the sword and the lance, but the bush-whack, the turf-cutter, the spade, and the bog-hoe, rusted with the blood of many a meadow, and begrimed with the dust of many a hard-fought field. . . . In Literature it is only the wild that attracts us. Dulness is but another name for tameness. It is the uncivilized free and wild thinking in "Hamlet" and the "Iliad," in all the Scriptures and Mythologies, not learned in the schools, that delights us. As the wild duck is more swift and beautiful than the tame, so is the wild—the mallard—thought. . . . A truly good book is something as natural, and as unexpectedly and unaccountably fair and perfect, as a wild flower discovered on the prairies of the West or in the jungles of the East. ("Walking," 64)

If we could stop thinking of language as something that distinguishes us from or in the order of nature, and start thinking of it as a craft by which we sense our connection to the earth, we could write wildly on behalf of wildness, and do it without hypocrisy. If we could learn to take comfort in the human, not for its dominance or its "humanity," but for the more-than-human fate and the web of connectedness that makes us what we are, gives us to speak, and pulls us toward one another and toward death, we could learn to let the world be. That would be a lesson of love.

INDEX